ISO 9001:2000
Explained

Second Edition

Also Available from ASQ Quality Press

The ISO Lesson Guide 2000: Pocket Guide to Q9001-2000, Second Edition
Dennis Arter and J.P. Russell

ISO 9001:2000—An Audio Workshop and Master Slide Presentation,
Second Edition
Charles A. Cianfrani and John E. (Jack) West

ISO 9000 at the Front Line
William A. Levinson

ISO 9001:2000 Quick Reference
Jeanne Ketola and Kathy Roberts

*Customer Satisfaction Measurement Simplified: A Step-by-Step Guide
for ISO 9001:2000 Certification*
Terry G. Vavra

The Practical Guide to People-Friendly Documentation
Adrienne Escoe

To request a complimentary catalog of ASQ Quality Press publications,
call 800-248-1946, or visit our Online Bookstore at
http://qualitypress.asq.org .

ISO 9001:2000 Explained

Second Edition

Charles A. Cianfrani
Joseph J. Tsiakals
John E. (Jack) West

ASQ Quality Press
Milwaukee, Wisconsin

ISO 9001:2000 Explained, Second Edition
Charles A. Cianfrani, Joseph J. Tsiakals, John E. (Jack) West

Library of Congress Cataloging-in-Publication Data

Cianfrani, Charles A.
  ISO 9001:2000 explained / Charles A. Cianfrani, Joseph J. Tsiakals, Jack West.--2nd ed.
  p. cm.
  Includes index.
  ISBN 0-87389-508-8 (alk. paper)
    1. ISO 9000 Series Standards. I. Tsiakals, Joseph J. II. West, Jack, 1944- III. Title.

TS156.6 .C45 2001
658.5'62--dc21   2001018852

10 9 8 7 6 5 4 3

ISBN 0-87389-508-8

Acquisitions Editor: Ken Zielske
Project Editor: Annemieke Koudstaal
Production Administrator: Gretchen Trautman
Special Marketing Representative: Matthew Meinholz

ASQ Mission: The American Society for Quality advances individual and organizational performance excellence worldwide by providing opportunities for learning, quality improvement, and knowledge exchange.

Attention: Bookstores, Wholesalers, Schools and Corporations:
ASQ Quality Press books, videotapes, audiotapes, and software are available at quantity discounts with bulk purchases for business, educational, or instructional use. For information, please contact ASQ Quality Press at 800-248-1946, or write to ASQ Quality Press, P.O. Box 3005, Milwaukee, WI 53201-3005.

To place orders or to request a free copy of the ASQ Quality Press Publications Catalog, including ASQ membership information, call 800-248-1946. Visit our web site at www.asq.org .

Printed in the United States of America

∞ Printed on acid-free paper

American Society for Quality

Quality Press
P.O. Box 3005
Milwaukee, Wisconsin 53201-3005
800-248-1946
Fax 414-272-1734
www.asq.org
http://qualitypress.asq.org
http://standardsgroup.asq.org

Contents

Preface

The ISO 9000 family of quality standards was initially issued in 1987, and a minor revision was issued in 1994. Over the past several years, the ISO technical committee responsible for this family has undertaken a major project to update the standards and to make them more user-friendly. ISO 9001:2000 is the second revision, but contains the first major changes to the standards since their initial issue. Some of the major changes include the following:

- Use of a process approach and a new structure for the standards that is built around a process model that considers all work in terms of inputs and outputs
- Shift in emphasis from preparing documented procedures to describe the system to developing and managing a family of effective processes
- Greater emphasis on the role of top management
- Increased emphasis on the customer, including understanding needs, meeting requirements, and measuring customer satisfaction
- Emphasis on setting measurable objectives and on measuring product and process performance
- Introduction of requirements for analysis and the use of data to define opportunities for improvement
- Formalization of the concept of continual improvement of the quality management system
- Use of wording that is more easily understood in all product sectors—not just hardware
- Provision via the application clause to adapt ISO 9001:2000 to all sizes and kinds of organizations and to all

sectors of the marketplace, which facilitates the elimination of ISO 9002 and ISO 9003

This book addresses the needs of the following:

- Individuals seeking a general understanding of the contents of ISO 9001:2000

- Organizations desiring guidance to facilitate the migration of an ISO 9001:1994–compliant quality management system to become compliant with ISO 9001:2000

- Organizations considering the use of ISO 9001:2000 as a foundation for the development of a comprehensive quality management system

- Educators who require a textbook to accompany a training class or course on the current quality management systems standards

This book explains the meaning and intent of the requirements of ISO 9001:2000 and discusses the requirements as they relate to each of the product categories. Where appropriate, it includes an elaboration of why the requirements are important. Key changes from the 1994 standard are identified. Finally, it includes a list of typical audit-type questions that an organization may consider to appraise compliance with the requirements.

Symbols are used to designate the following:

 Identifies changes from ISO 9001:1994 or new requirements in ISO 9001:2000

 Provides definitions of key terms used in ISO 9001:2000 as they are defined in ISO 9000:2000.

 Lists typical audit items to appraise compliance with the requirements of ISO 9001:2000

 Describes considerations for documentation

This book contains the text of ISO 9001:2000 as contained in the U.S. adoption of this standard. It also provides the ISO 9000:2000 definitions of key words and the text of the eight quality management principles as contained in the U.S. adoption of this standard.

The 2000 edition of ISO 9001 provides users with a much improved model for structuring and implementing a contemporary quality management system. This book facilitates an understanding of what the new standard says and what it means and how to apply it in any organization to achieve internal operating effectiveness and improved performance as viewed by customers.

CHAPTER

1

Introduction

0 INTRODUCTION

0.1 General

The adoption of a quality management system should be a strategic decision of an organization. The design and implementation of an organization's quality management system is influenced by varying needs, particular objectives, the products provided, the processes employed and the size and structure of the organization. It is not the intent of this International Standard to imply uniformity in the structure of quality management systems or uniformity of documentation.

The quality management system requirements specified in this International Standard are complementary to requirements for products. Information marked "NOTE" is for guidance in understanding or clarifying the associated requirement.

This International Standard can be used by internal and external parties, including certification bodies, to assess the organization's ability to meet customer, regulatory and the organization's own requirements.

The quality management principles stated in ISO 9000 and ISO 9004 have been taken into consideration during the development of this International Standard.

Source: ANSI/ISO/ASQ Q9001-2000

The introductory material in clause 0 and its subclauses is called "informative" in ISO language, meaning that it does not form part of the requirements of ISO 9001:2000. It exists to provide context, general understanding, and background.

This subclause discusses the intent of ISO 9001, the flexibility of the standard, and why organizations should use it. This can be summarized as follows:

- ISO 9001 contains the *requirements* for quality management systems.

- *Any organization* can use the standard to *demonstrate its ability* to meet customers', regulators', and the organization's own internal requirements.

- The standard can also be used *to assess* the organization's ability to meet customer requirements by the use of either internal or external parties (for example, a certification audit by a third-party accredited auditor, by a customer, or by internal auditors).
- ISO 9001 is very *flexible and does not imply uniformity* of quality management systems; as such, it does *not* imply a *requirement to change the structure* of quality management system documentation.

THE EIGHT QUALITY MANAGEMENT PRINCIPLES

Subclause 0.1 recognizes that ISO 9001 has been developed with the eight quality management principles given in ISO 9004 as a basis. While they help to form the foundation of ISO 9001, these principles do not appear in ISO 9001 and are not part of the requirements. They do appear in both ISO 9000 and ISO 9004. The principles as they appear in ISO 9000 are as follows:

"To lead and operate an organization successfully, it is necessary to direct and control it in a systematic and transparent manner. Success can result from implementing and maintaining a management system that is designed to continually improve performance while addressing the needs of all interested parties. Managing an organization encompasses quality management amongst other management disciplines.

Eight quality management principles have been identified that can be used by top management in order to lead the organization towards improved performance.

a) **Customer focus**
Organizations depend on their customers and therefore should understand current and future customer needs, should meet customer requirements and strive to exceed customer expectations.

b) **Leadership**

Leaders establish unity of purpose and direction of the organization. They should create and maintain the internal environment in which people can become fully involved in achieving the organization's objectives.

c) **Involvement of people**

People at all levels are the essence of an organization and their full involvement enables their abilities to be used for the organization's benefit.

d) **Process approach**

A desired result is achieved more efficiently when activities and related resources are managed as a process.

e) **System approach to management**

Identifying, understanding and managing interrelated processes as a system contributes to the organization's effectiveness and efficiency in achieving its objectives.

f) **Continual improvement**

Continual improvement of the organization's overall performance should be a permanent objective of the organization.

g) **Factual approach to decision making**

Effective decisions are based on the analysis of data and information.

h) **Mutually beneficial supplier relationships**

An organization and its suppliers are interdependent and a mutually beneficial relationship enhances the ability of both to create value.

These eight quality management principles form the basis for the quality management system standards within the ISO 9000 family."

Source: ANSI/ISO/ASQ Q9000-2000

0.2 Process approach

This International Standard promotes the adoption of a process approach when developing, implementing and improving the effectiveness of a quality management system, to enhance customer satisfaction by meeting customer requirements.

For an organization to function effectively, it has to identify and manage numerous linked activities. An activity using resources, and managed in order to enable the transformation of inputs into outputs, can be considered as a process. Often the output from one process directly forms the input to the next.

The application of a system of processes within an organization, together with the identification and interactions of these processes, and their management, can be referred to as the "process approach".

An advantage of the process approach is the ongoing control that it provides over the linkage between the individual processes within the system of processes, as well as over their combination and interaction.

When used within a quality management system, such an approach emphasizes the importance of

a) understanding and meeting requirements,

b) the need to consider processes in terms of added value,

c) obtaining results of process performance and effectiveness, and

d) continual improvement of processes based on objective measurement.

The model of a process-based quality management system shown in Figure 1 illustrates the process linkages presented in clauses 4 to 8. This illustration shows that customers play a significant role in defining requirements as inputs. Monitoring of customer satisfaction requires the evaluation of information relating to customer perception as to whether the organization has met the customer requirements. The model shown in Figure 1 covers all the requirements of this International Standard, but does not show processes at a detailed level.

NOTE   In addition, the methodology known as "Plan-Do-Check-Act" (PDCA) can be applied to all processes. PDCA can be briefly described as follows.

Plan: establish the objectives and processes necessary to deliver results in accordance with customer requirements and the organization's policies.

Do: implement the processes.

Check: monitor and measure processes and product against policies, objectives and requirements for the product and report the results.

Act: take actions to continually improve process performance.

Source: ANSI/ISO/ASQ Q9001-2000

Clause 0.2, *Process approach,* encourages organizations to base their quality management systems on the process concept. Figure 1 describes graphically one possible model of how the process approach applies to the quality management system. The text of clause 0.2 explains the model. Key concepts to remember from the clause include the following:

- Organizations will be more effective if they manage a system of interlinked processes. Identification and management of these processes can make the overall quality management system more effective in meeting customer requirements.

- The process approach itself is a very different way to understand the quality system than the understanding that is provided by the element approach (sometimes called the life-cycle model) used as the basis for ISO 9001:1994.

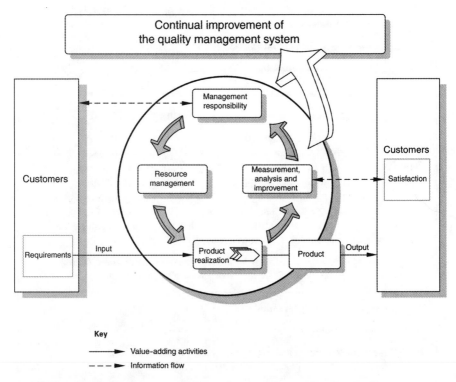

Figure 1   Model of a process-based quality management system
Source: ANSI/ISO/ASQ Q9001-2000

- The process approach has been adopted as a means to facilitate improvement.

- Figure 1 is not intended to reflect all of the processes in a quality management system. It is provided to enhance understanding and is not a part of the requirements.

- Figure 1 represents one model that can be used to describe how the process approach may be applied to quality management systems. There is no implication that Figure 1 is the ideal model or that it is the only model that can be used.

0.3 Relationship with ISO 9004

The present editions of ISO 9001 and ISO 9004 have been developed as a consistent pair of quality management system standards which have been designed to complement each other, but can also be used independently. Although the two International Standards have different scopes, they have similar structures in order to assist their application as a consistent pair.

ISO 9001 specifies requirements for a quality management system that can be used for internal application by organizations, or for certification, or for contractual purposes. It focuses on the effectiveness of the quality management system in meeting customer requirements.

ISO 9004 gives guidance on a wider range of objectives of a quality management system than does ISO 9001, particularly for the continual improvement of an organization's overall performance and efficiency, as well as its effectiveness. ISO 9004 is recommended as a guide for organizations whose top management wishes to move beyond the requirements of ISO 9001, in pursuit of continual improvement of performance. However, it is not intended for certification or for contractual purposes.

Source: ANSI/ISO/ASQ Q9001-2000

Clause 0.3 describes the relationship between the ISO 9001:2000 requirements document and ISO 9004:2000, which provides guidelines for a quality management system that is focused on performance improvement. Often identified as a "consistent pair" of quality management system standards, these two documents can be compared as follows:

- The two standards have very different scopes. ISO 9004 is not intended for certification or contractual use and it is not intended to provide guidance for implementing ISO 9001:2000. ISO 9004:2000 also is not intended to be used as a basis for auditing the quality management system.

- ISO 9004:2000 does provide guidance that can be used to improve the overall performance of the organization. To facilitate its use for improvement, its structure is consistent with that of ISO 9001:2000.

0.4 Compatibility with other management systems

This International Standard has been aligned with ISO 14001:1996 in order to enhance the compatibility of the two standards for the benefit of the user community.

This International Standard does not include requirements specific to other management systems, such as those particular to environmental management, occupational health and safety management, financial management or risk management. However, this International Standard enables an organization to align or integrate its own quality management system with related management system requirements. It is possible for an organization to adapt its existing management system(s) in order to establish a quality management system that complies with the requirements of this International Standard.

Source: ANSI/ISO/ASQ Q9001-2000

Clause 0.4, *Compatibility with other management systems,* states that the standard has been developed with the specific intent to be compatible with the ISO 14001:1996 *Environmental management systems—Specification with guidance for use.* In the opinion of most experts, there has always been good compatibility between ISO 14001:1996 and ISO 9001:1994. The drafters of the two families have worked together during the development of ISO 9001:2000 to ensure that this compatibility is maintained. In fact, experts from ISO TC 207, the

technical committee responsible for ISO 14001, were participants in the working group that drafted ISO 9001:2000.

Considerations related to compatibility include the
following:

- ISO 9001:2000 was structured to enhance its usability with
  ISO 14001.
- ISO 9001:2000 and ISO 14001:1996 can be used together
  without unnecessary duplication or conflicting requirements.
- Common requirements can form a basis for integrated
  management systems.
- Quality management system processes need not be estab-
  lished separately from an existing management system.

---

1 Scope

1.1 General

This International Standard specifies requirements for a quality
management system where an organization

a) needs to demonstrate its ability to consistently provide product
that meets customer and applicable regulatory requirements, and

b) aims to enhance customer satisfaction through the effective
application of the system, including processes for continual
improvement of the system and the assurance of conformity to
customer and applicable regulatory requirements.

NOTE In this International Standard, the term "product" applies only to
the product intended for, or required by, a customer.

Source: ANSI/ISO/ASQ Q9001-2000

Earlier it was indicated that clause 0 and its subclauses are
"informative" and do not form part of the requirements of
ISO 9001:2000. The scope is a normative part of the standard,
but the ISO directives also specify that the topics in clause 1
also must not contain requirements. Part 3 of the ISO directives states that the scope of a standard ". . . shall be succinct
so that it can be used as a summary for bibliographic purposes. This element shall be worded as a series of statements

of fact." Clause 1 therefore does not use the word *shall,* the keyword in ISO standards that makes a statement a requirement. As summarized in the following list, the scope contains material that describes how the standard is used.

- The intent is that ISO 9001:2000 be directly usable by all types and sizes of organizations regardless of product category.
- The scope makes it clear that an ISO 9001:2000–compliant quality management system is aimed at achieving customer satisfaction by meeting requirements.

ISO 9001:2000 is comprehensive in that it applies to all quality management system processes from the identification of requirements to the delivery and addressing of customer satisfaction.

1.2 Application

All requirements of this International Standard are generic and are intended to be applicable to all organizations, regardless of type, size and product provided.

Where any requirement(s) of this International Standard cannot be applied due to the nature of an organization and its product, this can be considered for exclusion.

Where exclusions are made, claims of conformity to this International Standard are not acceptable unless these exclusions are limited to requirements within clause 7, and such exclusions do not affect the organization's ability, or responsibility, to provide product that meets customer and applicable regulatory requirements.

Source: ANSI/ISO/ASQ Q9001-2000

The 1994 edition of the ISO 9000 family includes three requirement standards and a number of guidance documents. The 1994 requirement standards were as follows:

- ISO 9001, *Quality systems—Model for quality assurance in design/development, production, installation, and servicing*
- ISO 9002, *Quality systems—Model for quality assurance in production, installation, and servicing*
- ISO 9003, *Quality systems—Model for quality assurance in final inspection and test*

This arrangement provided a structure in which an organization could use the minimal ISO 9003 if it were appropriate to control only the detection and correction of nonconforming product. ISO 9002:1994 was intended for application by organizations where design and development were not performed by the organization.

ISO 9001:1994 was to be used when all aspects of design, production, installation, and servicing were applicable.

 ISO 9001:2000 eliminates the ISO 9002 and 9003 documents. The application subclause provides instructions on how to accommodate the elimination of ISO 9002 and ISO 9003. Key points of the application clause include the following:

- An organization can exclude requirements within clause 7 that are not required to meet customer requirements or are not required by the nature of the product or service provided.
- An organization cannot exclude requirements that affect the ability to provide conforming product or service.

Organizations have excluded activities covered by the 1994 editions when those activities were not performed and had no effect on conformity with customer requirements. Organizations typically use the quality manual to designate the requirements that are excluded. The new application clause only recognizes this reality.

On the other hand, many organizations that perform product design activities have used ANSI/ISO/ASQC Q9002-1994, which excludes design. With the new standard, this will not be acceptable. Organizations that perform design work and wish to achieve compliance with ISO 9001:2000 must address design requirements in their quality management systems based on ISO 9001:2000. The exclusions must be defined in the quality manual, but they do not absolve the organization of its responsibility to meet customer requirements.

Organizations need to exercise great care in excluding activities from their systems. The clause clearly states that an organization may not claim compliance with ISO 9001:2000 if quality management system exclusions exceed what is permitted in clause 1.2.

A second important aspect of the application clause is the relationship of ISO 9001:2000 to regulatory requirements. Regulations absolutely take precedence. This issue is critical to many users of the standard. Therefore, ISO 9001:2000 has been carefully developed to address regulatory needs. Today, ISO 9001:1994 is indicated in certain regulations as one approach for meeting the regulatory requirements for the design and production of various products. The intent of the application clause is to facilitate the continued use of ISO 9001:2000 by organizations that must address regulatory requirements.

When scope is reduced, regulatory requirements are still applicable. If scope is reduced further than permitted by the standard, the system is not ISO 9001:2000 compliant.

2 Normative reference

The following normative document contains provisions which, through reference in this text, constitute provisions of this International Standard. For dated references, subsequent amendments to, or revisions of, any of these publications do not apply. However, parties to agreements based on this International Standard are encouraged to investigate the possibility of applying the most recent edition of the normative document indicated below. For undated references, the latest edition of the normative document referred to applies. Members of ISO and IEC maintain registers of currently valid International Standards.

ISO 9000:2000, *Quality management systems—Fundamentals and vocabulary.*

3 Terms and definitions

For the purposes of this International Standard, the terms and definitions given in ISO 9000 apply.

The following terms, used in this edition of ISO 9001 to describe the supply chain, have been changed to reflect the vocabulary currently used:

supplier ——> organization ——> customer

The term "organization" replaces the term "supplier" used in ISO 9001:1994, and refers to the unit to which this International Standard applies. Also, the term "supplier" now replaces the term "subcontractor".

Throughout the text of this International Standard, wherever the term "product" occurs, it can also mean "service".

Source: ANSI/ISO/ASQ Q9001-2000

The only normative reference in ISO 9001:2000 is ISO 9000: 2000, which contains the terms and definitions used in the ISO 9000 family. The only normative content of ISO 9000:2000 is the actual definitions. Key points from clauses 2 and 3 include the following:

- ISO 9000:2000 contains definitions that are normative and form part of the requirements.

- Supply-chain terminology is used to be consistent with language that is commonly used in the ordinary course of operations:

    supplier ⟶ organization ⟶ customer

- Wherever the term *product* is used, it can also mean service.

CHAPTER

2

Quality Management System and General Documentation

4 Quality management system

4.1 General requirements

The organization shall establish, document, implement and maintain a quality management system and continually improve its effectiveness in accordance with the requirements of this International Standard.

The organization shall

a) identify the processes needed for the quality management system and their application throughout the organization (see 1.2),

b) determine the sequence and interaction of these processes,

c) determine criteria and methods needed to ensure that both the operation and control of these processes are effective,

d) ensure the availability of resources and information necessary to support the operation and monitoring of these processes,

e) monitor, measure and analyse these processes, and

f) implement actions necessary to achieve planned results and continual improvement of these processes.

These processes shall be managed by the organization in accordance with the requirements of this International Standard.

Where an organization chooses to outsource any process that affects product conformity with requirements, the organization shall ensure control over such processes. Control of such outsourced processes shall be identified within the quality management system.

NOTE   Processes needed for the quality management system referred to above should include processes for management activities, provision of resources, product realization and measurement.

Source: ANSI/ISO/ASQ Q9001-2000

The basic requirement for a quality management system is that the organization must identify and manage the family of processes needed to ensure conformity. The quality management system ensures compliance with the quality policy and ensures that quality objectives are met. Organizations should not lose sight of this basic concept. It is easy to get so absorbed in documenting a system that the basic concept is lost. While documentation is important, the primary emphasis should be on developing and implementing effective quality management system processes.

It is critical to understand the difference between managing a system and documenting a system. Clause 4.1 does not directly address documentation. Rather, clause 4.1 requires that processes be developed and implemented to make up the overall system. It also requires that processes be managed and continually improved. These improvement activities must include monitoring, measurement, and analysis of the processes. This is at the heart of the *process approach* and represents one of the major changes in focus from ISO 9001:1994.

The activities that organizations will need to consider include the following:

- Identification of processes and their interrelationships, sequences, and interactions
- Establishment of criteria and means to effectively operate, monitor, measure, analyze, and control the processes
- Improvement of quality management system effectiveness including improvement of these processes
- Achievement of control of quality management system processes that are outsourced to another organization that affect product conformity

Understanding and using this *process approach* is critical to compliance with ISO 9001:2000 because, as we will see in the next section, the requirements for documented procedures have been dramatically reduced.

 DEFINITIONS

Management system (3.2.2)—**system** (3.2.1) to establish policy and objectives and to achieve those objectives

NOTE   A management system of an **organization** (3.3.1) can include different management systems, such as a **quality management system** (3.2.3), a financial management system or an environmental management system.

Organization (3.3.1)—group of people and facilities with an arrangement of responsibilities, authorities and relationships

EXAMPLE   Company, corporation, firm, enterprise, institution, charity, sole trader, association, or parts or combination thereof.

NOTE 1   The arrangement is generally orderly.

NOTE 2   An organization can be public or private.

NOTE 3   This definition is valid for the purposes of **quality management system** (3.2.3) standards. The term "organization" is defined differently in ISO/IEC Guide 2.

Process (3.4.1)—set of interrelated or interacting activities which transforms inputs into outputs

NOTE 1   Inputs to a process are generally outputs of other processes.

NOTE 2   Processes in an **organization** (3.3.1) are generally planned and carried out under controlled conditions to add value.

NOTE 3   A process where the **conformity** (3.6.1) of the resulting **product** (3.4.2) cannot be readily or economically verified is frequently referred to as a "special process".

Quality (3.1.1)—degree to which a set of inherent **characteristics** (3.5.1) fulfils **requirements** (3.1.2)

NOTE 1   The term "quality" can be used with adjectives such as poor, good or excellent.

NOTE 2   "Inherent", as opposed to "assigned", means existing in something, especially as a permanent characteristic.

Quality management system (3.2.3)—**management system** (3.2.2) to direct and control an **organization** (3.3.1) with regard to **quality** (3.1.1)

Requirement (3.1.2)—need or expectation that is stated, generally implied or obligatory

NOTE 1   "Generally implied" means that it is custom or common practice for the **organization** (3.3.1), its **customers** (3.3.5) and other **interested parties** (3.3.7), that the need or expectation under consideration is implied.

NOTE 2   A qualifier can be used to denote a specific type of requirement, e.g. product requirement, quality management requirement, customer requirement.

NOTE 3   A specified requirement is one which is stated, for example, in a **document** (3.7.2).

NOTE 4   Requirements can be generated by different interested parties.

Source: ANSI/ISO/ASQ Q9000-2000

 # TYPICAL AUDIT ITEMS FOR COMPLIANCE

Items representing a difference from ISO 9001:1994 have a Δ at the end.

- Have the processes needed for quality management been identified? Δ
- Have sequence and interaction of these processes been determined? Δ
- Have criteria and control methods been determined for control of the processes in the quality management system? Δ
- Is information available to support the operation and monitoring of the processes? Δ
- Are processes measured, monitored, and analyzed with appropriate actions taken to achieve planned results and continual improvement? Δ
- Is the quality management system established, documented, implemented, maintained, and continually improved? Δ
- Has provision been made to ensure control of quality management system processes that are outsourced? Δ

4.2 Documentation requirements

4.2.1 General

The quality management system documentation shall include

a) documented statements of a quality policy and quality objectives,

b) a quality manual,

c) documented procedures required by this International Standard,

d) documents needed by the organization to ensure the effective planning, operation and control of its processes, and

e) records required by this International Standard (see 4.2.4).

NOTE 1   Where the term "documented procedure" appears within this International Standard, this means that the procedure is established, documented, implemented and maintained.

NOTE 2   The extent of the quality management system documentation can differ from one organization to another due to

a) the size of organization and type of activities,

b) the complexity of processes and their interactions, and

c) the competence of personnel.

NOTE 3   The documentation can be in any form or type of medium.

Source: ANSI/ISO/ASQ Q9001-2000

Documentation forms a basis for understanding the system, communicating its processes and requirements within the organization, describing it to other organizations, and determining the effectiveness of implementation. The organization is required to establish, document, maintain, and improve the quality management system. It is top management's responsibility to facilitate the establishment of the system. Top management must also ensure that the system is actually implemented; it is obviously insufficient to have a documented system that is not implemented. The documented system must reflect activities that are actually performed to ensure conformity.

On the other hand, the perceived requirement for an excessive number of documented procedures has been one of the most criticized aspects of ISO 9001:1994. ISO 9001:2000 makes a significant step toward changing that perception. The emphasis has shifted from documenting procedures that address 20 elements to managing a system of processes to achieve specific quality objectives. It is the process management described earlier that is important. Organizations have always had the freedom to determine the extent of documentation that is appropriate. With ISO 9001:2000 they will now have even more flexibility to select documentation methods and structures that are appropriate for the organization's needs.

The system must also be maintained. Nothing is static; changes occur constantly in most organizations. This means the system must be used on an ongoing basis and must be kept current.

The extent of the quality management system documentation for an organization depends on the organization's situation. As a minimum, the documentation must include an appropriate combination of the following documents:

- *Documents* describing the *quality policy* required by clause 5.3 and giving the *quality objectives* required by clause 5.4.1.

- The *quality manual* must describe the interaction of the processes in the quality management system. ISO 9001:2000 requires that the organization have a quality manual and that the manual meet certain requirements. The details of these requirements are given in clause 4.2.2 and will be discussed later in this chapter. The manual must either contain or reference the documented procedures related to the system's processes.

- There must be *documented procedures* that describe the system. These documents must either be included as a part of or be referenced in the quality manual. ISO 9001:2000 specifically requires "documented procedures" in only six places, but remember that the organization must also have documentation of the system's processes and their interactions. Once the processes of the quality management system have been defined and their interactions established, the key processes should be described in documented procedures. Along with the quality manual, these documented procedures provide a mechanism for communication of the processes to the organization. A well-prepared quality manual along with easily understood documented procedures will help to ensure that all employees understand the quality management system. Many organizations will choose to maintain their quality manual and other quality system documentation in electronic format, so the distinction between one comprehensive quality manual that includes all quality system documentation and a quality manual that references additional documentation becomes academic.

It may come as a surprise to many that ISO 9001:2000 has far fewer specific requirements for documented procedures than ISO 9001:1994. Table 2.1 illustrates the differences. It is important to remember that clause 4.2.1d requires the organization to identify and prepare any documents necessary for the effective planning, operation, and control of its processes. Organizations typically need additional documentation to fully describe the quality management system beyond the six explicitly required documented procedures.

- Other *system documentation* is required as necessary to document the sequences and activities required for the operation of the system. In addition to the quality manual and the documented procedures that describe the overall processes of the quality management system, organizations are specifically required to prepare other documentation needed for control of processes. The type and extent of these documents must be determined by the organization. This documentation is typically in the form of written procedures or work instructions. Table 2.2 provides a listing of the clauses in ISO 9001:2000 where such documentation is discussed or required.

TABLE 2.1 Comparison of requirements for documented procedures.

ANSI/ISO/ASQ Q9001-2000		ANSI/ISO/ASQC Q9001-1994	
Clause	Documented Procedure Required	Clause	Documented Procedure Required
		4.3.1	Contract review
		4.4.1	Design control
4.2.3	Control of documents	4.5	Document and data control
		4.6.1	Purchasing
		4.7	Customer–supplied product
		4.8	Product identification and traceability
		4.9	Process control
		4.10.1	Inspection and testing
		4.11.1	Control of measuring and test equipment
		4.12	Inspection and test status
8.3	Control of nonconforming product	4.13.1	Control of nonconforming product
8.5.2	Corrective action	4.14.1	Corrective and preventive action
8.5.3	Preventive action	4.14.1	Corrective and preventive action
		4.15.1	Handling, storage, packaging, preservation, and delivery
4.2.4	Control of records	4.16	Control of quality records
8.2.2	Internal quality audits	4.17	Internal quality audits
		4.18	Training
		4.19	Servicing
		4.20	Statistical techniques

TABLE 2.2 Requirements for documentation other than specifically required documented procedures and records.

ANSI/ISO/ASQ Q9001-2000 Clause	Requirements for Documentation Other than Specifically Required Documented Procedures and Records
4.1[1]	"The organization shall establish, document, . . . a quality management system . . ."
4.2.1[1]	". . . quality management system documentation shall include:
	a) . . . quality policy and quality objectives . . .
	b) . . . quality manual . . .
	d) . . . documents required by the organization to ensure the effective operation and control of its processes. . . ."
	e) quality records.
7.1[1]	". . . in planning product realization, the organization shall determine the following . . . b) need to establish processes, documents, and . . . "
7.3.3[1]	Design output "provided in a form that enables verification"
7.5.1[1]	b) "availability of work instructions as necessary"

[1]Requirement for documentation but no direct reference to clause 4.2.3.

For example, in clause 5.3 there is no requirement to create a documented procedure for describing the process of creating a quality policy. However, the organization must have a quality policy, and this quality policy is a document that needs to be controlled. This means that processes must ensure that the most current version of the quality policy has been issued and that obsolete versions have been removed or appropriately marked as such. It would be confusing to have obsolete versions of an organization's quality policy still present within the organization.

Organizations have many options for documenting their systems. Note, for example, that the quality manual need not be a separate document. Systems can be developed where the manual contains documented procedures. In fact, for a small organization it may be appropriate to include most or all of the system documentation in a single manual. Depending on the size and complexity of the organization, it may also be appropriate that the documents describing the sequences and interactions of processes be combined with the documented procedures that describe the system. Certainly other combinations are possible. Remember that the extent of required documentation depends on the following:

- Size and type of organization
- Complexity and interaction of the organization's processes
- Competency of the organization's people

Organizations may use any form or media for any of the documents in the quality management system. This means that the quality manual, the documented procedures, and the other documents of the system may be published in any way the organization chooses; there are no restrictions. However, the organization must remember in selecting its documentation media that the document control provisions of clause 4.2.3 must be met.

 DEFINITIONS

Document (3.7.2)—**information** (3.7.1) and its supporting medium

EXAMPLE   **Record** (3.7.6), **specification** (3.7.3), procedure document, drawing, report, standard.

NOTE 1   The medium can be paper, magnetic, electronic or optical computer disc, photograph or master sample, or a combination thereof.

NOTE 2   A set of documents, for example specifications and records, is frequently called "documentation".

NOTE 3   Some **requirements** (3.1.2) (e.g. the requirement to be readable) relate to all types of documents, however there can be different requirements for specifications (e.g. the requirement to be revision controlled) and records (e.g. the requirement to be retrievable).

Procedure (3.4.5)—specified way to carry out an activity or a **process** (3.4.1)

NOTE 1 Procedures can be documented or not.

NOTE 2 When a procedure is documented, the term "written procedure" or "documented procedure" is frequently used. The **document** (3.7.2) that contains a procedure can be called a "procedure document".

Source: ANSI/ISO/ASQ Q9000-2000

 # TYPICAL AUDIT ITEMS FOR COMPLIANCE

Items representing a difference from ISO 9001:1994 have a Δ at the end.

- Have documented procedures been prepared where specifically required by ISO 9001:2000 (see Table 2.1)? Δ
- Is the extent of quality management system documentation dependent on the size and type of the organization? Δ
- Is the extent of quality management system documentation dependent on the complexity and interaction of processes in the organization? Δ
- Is the extent of quality management system documentation dependent on the competence of personnel in the organization?

4.2.2 Quality manual

The organization shall establish and maintain a quality manual that includes

a) the scope of the quality management system, including details of and justification for any exclusions (see 1.2),

b) the documented procedures established for the quality management system, or reference to them, and

c) a description of the interaction between the processes of the quality management system.

Source: ANSI/ISO/ASQ Q9001-2000

The quality manual is the document that describes the overall quality management system, its processes, and the interrelationship among those processes. It can either contain or reference more detailed documented procedures. The manual should be useful to facilitate understanding of the quality management system, and the organization should not feel constrained to a specific format for the manual's content. The format and content should be developed in a way that describes how the organization's quality management system really works.

 While ISO 9001:1994 required a description of how the system is documented, ISO 9001:2000 requires the manual to have a description of the "interaction between" the processes that make up the system. Note this difference in focus.

 There is a new requirement in clause 4.2.2a that the quality manual include the scope of the quality management system, including the details of and justification for any exclusions the organization has taken under clause 1.2, *Application.*

 ## DEFINITIONS

Quality (3.1.1)—degree to which a set of inherent **characteristics** (3.5.1) fulfils **requirements** (3.1.2)

NOTE 1   The term "quality" can be used with adjectives such as poor, good or excellent.

NOTE 2   "Inherent", as opposed to "assigned", means existing in something, especially as a permanent characteristic.

Quality management system (3.2.3)—**management system** (3.2.2) to direct and control an **organization** (3.3.1) with regard to **quality** (3.1.1)

Quality manual (3.7.4)—**document** (3.7.2) specifying the **quality management system** (3.2.3) of an **organization** (3.3.1)

NOTE   Quality manuals can vary in detail and format to suit the size and complexity of an individual organization.

Source: ANSI/ISO/ASQ Q9000-2000

TYPICAL AUDIT ITEMS FOR COMPLIANCE

Items representing a difference from ISO 9001:1994 have a Δ at the end.

- Does the organization have a quality manual that describes the interaction of the processes in the quality management system? Δ

- Does the quality manual either include or reference the documented procedures describing the processes of the quality management system?

- Does the quality manual include the scope of the quality management system, including details of and justification for any exclusions taken under clause 1.2? Δ

- Is the quality manual a controlled document?

4.2.3 Control of documents

Documents required by the quality management system shall be controlled. Records are a special type of document and shall be controlled according to the requirements given in 4.2.4.

A documented procedure shall be established to define the controls needed

a) to approve documents for adequacy prior to issue,

b) to review and update as necessary and re-approve documents,

c) to ensure that changes and the current revision status of documents are identified,

d) to ensure that relevant versions of applicable documents are available at points of use,

e) to ensure that documents remain legible and readily identifiable,

f) to ensure that documents of external origin are identified and their distribution controlled, and

g) to prevent the unintended use of obsolete documents, and to apply suitable identification to them if they are retained for any purpose.

Source: ANSI/ISO/ASQ Q9001-2000

4.2.4 Control of records

Records shall be established and maintained to provide evidence of conformity to requirements and of the effective operation of the quality management system. Records shall remain legible, readily identifiable and retrievable. A documented procedure shall be established to define the controls needed for the identification, storage, protection, retrieval, retention time and disposition of records.

Source: ANSI/ISO/ASQ Q9001-2000

Documents that are part of the quality management system must be controlled to ensure that correct requirements are available. Controls for documents must include a number of specific activities.

Approval prior to issue for use is required to ensure that documents are adequate. Written document control procedures should specify how this approval is accomplished. Many organizations find it worthwhile to include a process for internal review of the documents by all affected units of the organizations as part of the pre-issue review process.

 Review, updating, and reapproval are required as necessary. ISO 9001:1994 required that changes in documents be reviewed and reapproved. ISO 9001:2000 adds the concept that the documents themselves must be reviewed. Some organizations create systems to ensure that documents are reviewed for continued suitability on a periodic, scheduled basis. There is no stated requirement that the review be periodic or scheduled, just that it occur as necessary. If the documentation system is vibrant and its documents are used daily, it may prove sufficient to conduct the reviews only when there is a known need to make a change. Each organization should define a document review, revision, and reapproval process that suits its own business needs.

Controls are required to ensure that the correct revisions of documents are identified and available at the points of use, including controls (such as identification) to prevent unintended use of obsolete documents. Many organizations have migrated to computer-based processes for tracking the current issue of documents. Also, means are required to ensure that documents remain legible, retrievable, and readily identifiable.

And controls must extend to documents of external origin, such as industry and customer specifications and standards.

A record is a special type of document and has its own control requirements. Records are documents that provide evidence that an activity has been accomplished or that an event has happened. Records are also used to provide information on the condition (such as conformity or nonconformity) of a product. While the other types of documents in the quality management system may indicate what is to be done (the current and future action), records provide evidence of what has occurred (past action).

As with documented procedures, there has been a shift in the emphasis of the record requirements. ISO 9001:2000 has somewhat more emphasis on the organization defining the required records rather than specifying them in the standards. Table 2.3 gives a listing of the specified record requirements as well as the requirements for the organization to identify its own record needs.

TABLE 2.3 Record-related requirements.

ANSI/ISO/ASQ Q9001-2000		ANSI/ISO/ASQC Q9001-1994	
Clause	*Record-Related Requirement*	*Clause*	*Record-Related Requirement*
4.2.1	Quality management system documentation including "e) records required by this international standard"		
4.2.3	"records are a special type of document and shall be controlled . . . 4.2.4."		

(Continued)

TABLE 2.3   Continued.

ANSI/ISO/ASQ Q9001-2000		ANSI/ISO/ASQC Q9001-1994	
Clause	*Record-Related Requirement*	*Clause*	*Record-Related Requirement*
$4.2.4^2$	"Records shall be established and maintained to provide evidence of conformity."	4.16^2	Records shall be maintained to demonstrate conformance to specified requirements and the effective operation of the quality system; pertinent quality records from the subcontractor shall be an element of these data.
		$4.10.5^2$	Establish and maintain records that provide evidence that the product has been inspected and/or tested.
$5.5.2^3$	The management representative reports to top management on performance of the quality management system.		
5.6.1	Management review	4.1.3	Management review
		4.16^1	Retention time for quality records . . . recorded
6.2.2	Education, training, skills, and experience.	4.18	Records of training
$7.1.d^2$	The records that are necessary ". . . to provide evidence that the realizaton processes and resulting product meet requirements."	$4.10.1^2$	Records to be established shall be detailed in the quality plan or documented procedures
7.2.2	Records of review of requirements related to the product requirements	4.3.4	Records of contract review

(Continued)

TABLE 2.3 Continued.

ANSI/ISO/ASQ Q9001-2000		ANSI/ISO/ASQC Q9001-1994	
Clause	Record-Related Requirement	Clause	Record-Related Requirement
7.3.2	Records of inputs to product Requirements in design and development		
7.3.4	Records of design and development review and follow-up actions	4.4.6	Records of design reviews
7.3.5	Records of the design and development verification and subsequent follow-up actions	4.4.7	The design-verification measures shall be recorded
7.3.6	Records of the design and development validation and subsequent follow-up actions		
7.3.7	Design and development changes ". . . identified and records maintained . . . Records of result of review of change and any required actions. . . ."	4.4.9	"design changes . . . documented reviewed . . . before implementation"
7.4.1	Records of supplier evaluation results and follow-up actions	4.6.2c	Establish and maintain quality records of acceptable subcontractors
		4.10.2.3	Incoming product is released for urgent production purposes; prior to verification, it shall be positively identified and recorded.
7.5.2d^2	Requirements for records related to process validation	4.9	Records shall be maintained for qualified processes, equipment, and personnel, as appropriate.
7.5.3	Record of unique product identification, (where traceability is a requirement)	4.8	Unique identification of individual product or batches, where traceability is a requirement

(Continued)

TABLE 2.3 Continued.

ANSI/ISO/ASQ Q9001-2000		ANSI/ISO/ASQC Q9001-1994	
Clause	Record-Related Requirement	Clause	Record-Related Requirement
7.5.4	Records of any customer property that is lost, damaged or otherwise found unsuitable	4.7	Any customer or supplier product that is lost, damaged, or is otherwise unsuitable for use shall be recorded and reported to the customer.
7.6.a[1]	The basis used for calibration	4.11.2b[1]	The basis used for calibration
7.6[1]	Record validity of previous measurement results when equipment is found outside of requirements.	4.11.2f[1]	Document validity of previous results when equipment is found to be out of calibration
7.6[1]	Results of calibration and verification	4.11.1	Shall maintain records as evidence of control of calibration checks
		4.11.2e	Calibration records for inspection, measuring, and test equipment
7.6.c[3]	Be identified to enable calibration status to be identified	4.11.2d[1]	Suitable indicator or approved identification record to show calibration status
8.2.2[2]	Audit records	4.17	Results of the audits shall be recorded.
8.2.2	Follow-up audit actions include reporting of verification results (see 8.5.2)	4.17	Follow-up audit activities shall verify and record the implementation and effectiveness of the corrective action taken.
8.2.4	Evidence of conformity with the acceptance criteria; records shall indicate the authority responsible for release of product.	4.10.5[2]	Records shall identify the inspection authority responsible for the release of product.

(Continued)

TABLE 2.3 Continued.

ANSI/ISO/ASQ Q9001-2000		ANSI/ISO/ASQC Q9001-1994	
Clause	Record-Related Requirement	Clause	Record-Related Requirement
8.3	Record of nature of nonconformity, action taken, and any concessions	4.13.1[1]	". . . controls shall provide for . . . documentation . . ."
8.3	Record of any concessions obtained	4.13.2	Description of nonconformity that has been accepted by customer and descriiption of repairs shall be recorded to denote the actual condition.
		4.14.1[1]	Record any changes to the documented procedures resulting from corrective and preventive action.
		4.14.2b	Investigation of the cause of nonconformities relating to product, process, and quality system and recording the results of the investigation
8.5.2e	Record results of corrective actions taken.		
8.5.3d	Record results of preventive actions taken.		

[1]Apparent direct requirement for a record but no reference to clause 4.2.4 of ISO 9001:2000 or clause 4.16 of ANSI/ISO/ASQC Q9001-1994

[2]Requirement for a process or procedure to define quality records to be kept; may not reference clause 4.2.4 of ISO 9001:2000 or clause 4.16 of ANSI/ISO/ASQC Q9001-1994

[3]Requirement for "reporting" or reporting of results; may or may not involve quality records. No reference to clause 4.2.4 of ISO 9001:2000 or clause 4.16 of ANSI/ISO/ASQC Q9001-1994

Organizations must identify the records to be retained along with the length of time each type of record must be retained. Many organizations do not have lengthy retention times and need only provide for the normal filing of records.

In such cases, the documented procedure can be very simple, with a matrix giving the information required. Other organizations have very long retention times for some records and need to consider long-term indexing and retrieval from off-site archives. For all cases, controls should be appropriate to the circumstances and the retention times needed.

Organizations also need to identify the storage conditions and protection required for the records that they maintain. It is particularly important to consider how the organization would be affected if the records became lost or were destroyed. Organizations should look at each type of record and determine appropriate protection based on importance to the continued operation of the quality management system. For many noncritical records, storage in normal file cabinets may be appropriate. Critical records should be protected from potential fire and other damage. Provisions need to be made for backup of records stored on magnetic media and for appropriate protection of the backup copies. In the event of a fire, it will do little good to have computer backup files stored on a shelf next to the computer. Although not a requirement of ISO 9001, many organizations create and maintain a disaster recovery plan to address such situations.

 DEFINITIONS

Document (3.7.2)—information (3.7.1) and its supporting medium

EXAMPLE   **Record** (3.7.6), **specification** (3.7.3), procedure document, drawing, report, standard.

NOTE 1   The medium can be paper, magnetic, electronic or optical computer disc, photograph or master sample, or a combination thereof.

NOTE 2   A set of documents, for example specifications and records, is frequently called "documentation".

NOTE 3   Some **requirements** (3.1.2) (e.g. the requirement to be readable) relate to all types of documents, however there can be different requirements for specifications (e.g. the requirement to be revision controlled) and records (e.g. the requirement to be retrievable).

Procedure (3.4.5)—specified way to carry out an activity or a **process** (3.4.1)

NOTE 1 Procedures can be documented or not.

NOTE 2 When a procedure is documented, the term "written procedure" or "documented procedure" is frequently used. The **document** (3.7.2) that contains a procedure can be called a "procedure document".

Quality (3.1.1)—degree to which a set of inherent **characteristics** (3.5.1) fulfils **requirements** (3.1.2)

NOTE 1 The term "quality" can be used with adjectives such as poor, good or excellent.

NOTE 2 "Inherent", as opposed to "assigned", means existing in something, especially as a permanent characteristic

Quality management system (3.2.3)—**management system** (3.2.2) to direct and control an **organization** (3.3.1) with regard to **quality** (3.1.1)

Record (3.7.6)—**document** (3.7.2) stating results achieved or providing evidence of activities performed

NOTE 1 Records can be used, for example, to document **traceability** (3.5.4) and to provide evidence of **verification** (3.8.4), **preventive action** (3.6.4) and **corrective action** (3.6.5).

NOTE 2 Generally records need not be under revision control.

Review (3.8.7)—activity undertaken to determine the suitability, adequacy and **effectiveness** (3.2.14) of the subject matter to achieve established objectives

NOTE Review can also include the determination of **efficiency** (3.2.15).

EXAMPLE   Management review, design and development review, review of customer requirements and nonconformity review.

Source: ANSI/ISO/ASQ Q9000-2000

 # CONSIDERATIONS FOR DOCUMENTATION

There must be a documented procedure to describe how document control is accomplished, and it must include the requirements of clauses 4.2.3a through 4.2.3g. There also must be a documented procedure for the control of quality records covering the items listed in clause 4.2.4. Since control considerations for records are different from those for other documents, a separate documented procedure is required for the control of records.

TYPICAL AUDIT ITEMS FOR COMPLIANCE

Items representing a difference from ISO 9001:1994 have a Δ at the end.

Audit items related to control of documents (except quality records)

- Has a documented procedure been established for document control?
- Are documents approved for adequacy prior to use?
- Are documents reviewed and updated as necessary? Δ
- Are document changes reapproved to ensure adequacy prior to use?
- Is current document revision status maintained?
- Are relevant versions of applicable documents available at points of use?
- Is there a process to ensure that documents remain legible, readily identifiable, and retrievable?
- Are documents of external origin identified and their distribution controlled?
- Are obsolete documents retained for any purpose suitably identified to prevent unintended use?

Audit items related to control of records

- Is there a documented procedure for the control of records?
- Have the organization's records been identified?
- Have retention times and disposition requirements been determined for all records?
- Are records disposed of as required by the organization's documented procedures?
- Have storage and retrieval requirements been determined and implemented for records?
- Have protection requirements been determined and implemented for records?

CHAPTER

3

Management Responsibility

5 Management responsibility

5.1 Management commitment

Top management shall provide evidence of its commitment to the development and implementation of the quality management system and continually improving its effectiveness by

a) communicating to the organization the importance of meeting customer as well as statutory and regulatory requirements,

b) establishing the quality policy,

c) ensuring that quality objectives are established,

d) conducting management reviews, and

e) ensuring the availability of resources.

5.2 Customer focus

Top management shall ensure that customer requirements are determined and are met with the aim of enhancing customer satisfaction (see 7.2.1 and 8.2.1).

Source: ANSI/ISO/ASQ Q9001-2000

Top management commitment is now required not only to develop the quality management system but also to continually improve its effectiveness.

Top management must demonstrate commitment by conducting specific activities. It is not sufficient for top managers merely to proclaim their commitment. There are specific responsibilities that must be fulfilled. Some of these responsibilities were required of top managers by the 1994 version of ISO 9001; others may well have been delegated. As with the 1994 version, top management must provide resources and must perform management reviews. They must also be actively involved in ensuring that the quality policy and objectives are established. Active participation of senior leaders in the development and deployment of both the quality policy and related objectives is a must for attaining compliance.

ISO 9001:2000 includes two new requirements in this clause. In addition to communicating the organization's policy and goals as required by the 1994 version, top management must communicate to the organization the importance of meeting customer requirements and regulatory and statutory requirements. There must be a process not only to create awareness of the organization's quality policy and quality objectives but also to maintain this awareness. Leaders demonstrate this commitment by both words and actions.

 Top management must ensure that customer requirements are determined, understood, and met. Top managers are not expected to accomplish all of this on their own, but they must be able to demonstrate that they have processes to ensure that these requirements are met.

 DEFINITIONS

Customer (3.3.5)—**organization** (3.3.1) or person that receives a **product** (3.4.2)

EXAMPLE   Consumer, client, end-user, retailer, beneficiary and purchaser.
NOTE   A   customer   can   be   internal   or   external   to   the organization.

Management system (3.2.2)—**system** (3.2.1) to establish policy and objectives and to achieve those objectives

NOTE   A management system of an **organization** (3.3.1) can include different management systems, such as a **quality management system** (3.2.3), a financial management system or an environmental management system.

Organization (3.3.1)—group of people and facilities with an arrangement of responsibilities, authorities and relationships

EXAMPLE   Company, corporation, firm, enterprise, institution, charity, sole trader, association, or parts or combination thereof.
NOTE 1   The arrangement is generally orderly.
NOTE 2   An organization can be public or private.
NOTE 3   This definition is valid for the purposes of **quality management system** (3.2.3) standards. The term "organization" is defined differently in ISO/IEC Guide 2.

Quality (3.1.1)—degree to which a set of inherent **characteristics** (3.5.1) fulfils **requirements** (3.1.2)

NOTE 1   The term "quality" can be used with adjectives such as poor, good or excellent.
NOTE 2   "Inherent", as opposed to "assigned", means existing in something, especially as a permanent characteristic.

Quality management system (3.2.3)—**management system** (3.2.2) to direct and control an **organization** (3.3.1) with regard to **quality** (3.1.1)

Top management (3.2.7)—person or group of people who directs and controls an **organization** (3.3.1) at the highest level

Source: ANSI/ISO/ASQ Q9000-2000

CONSIDERATIONS FOR DOCUMENTATION

Although not specifically required, organizations should consider documenting their processes to communicate customer, regulatory, and legal requirements. This clause does not require any specific quality records.

TYPICAL AUDIT ITEMS FOR COMPLIANCE

Items representing a difference from ISO 9001:1994 have a Δ at the end.

- Has top management established quality policy?
- Has top management developed quality objectives?
- Do top managers regularly perform management reviews and assess opportunities for improvement?
- Does top management provide and regularly review the adequacy of resources?
- Is top management involved in the process to determine customer requirements and to ensure that they are met? Δ
- Is there a process to ensure that employees understand the importance of meeting customer, regulatory, and statutory requirements? Δ
- Is there evidence of top management commitment to continually improve QMS effectiveness? Δ

5.3 Quality policy

Top management shall ensure that the quality policy

a) is appropriate to the purpose of the organization,

b) includes a commitment to comply with requirements and continually improve the effectiveness of the quality management system,

c) provides a framework for establishing and reviewing quality objectives,

d) is communicated and understood within the organization, and

e) is reviewed for continuing suitability

Source: ANSI/ISO/ASQ Q9001-2000

Clause 5.1 requires that top management establish the quality policy. Clause 5.3 elaborates on the substance of the policy. The clause has three requirements for the content of the policy itself and two requirements that deal with how it is to be communicated and reviewed.

The policy must first be appropriate to the needs of the organization and its customers. This means that the organization should not adopt a policy that it cannot carry out. The organization must have both the capability and the dedication required to implement the policy. It will do no good to create a policy with lofty goals if it is impossible for the organization to meet those goals. On the other hand, the policy must also meet the needs of the organization's customers, which is a basic concept of ISO 9001. In developing the policy, it is important to think through the elements of policy needed to meet customer needs. The needs can then be defined in terms of the key processes or activities of the organization.

 Clause 5.3 specifies two basic requirements that the policy must meet. It must include commitment to meeting

requirements and commitment to improving the effectiveness of the quality management system. Although meeting requirements was a fundamental of ISO 9001:1994, specific reference to improvement of the quality management system is new. Meeting requirements and improvement are foundations of the system, and there must be a commitment to both of these concepts.

There is a new emphasis on the concept of continual improvement. Improvement is not new; the 1994 version of ISO 9001 has requirements to use corrective and preventive actions as a means for improvement, and these concepts are retained. With ISO 9001:2000, the organization must plan its activities for improvement, and the measurable objectives of the organization must be set with improvement in mind. Measurement, collection, and analysis of data are required for identifying areas for improvement. This process of improving the effectiveness of meeting the requirements of the quality management system must be done on a continual basis through methods such as periodic management reviews.

 The quality policy must create the framework for setting and reviewing objectives, and the framework should be appropriate to the needs of the organization. It must also provide for the establishment of objectives at the various levels and functions of the organization. The standard requires this to be done at "relevant functions and levels." Organizations must define what this means for them. In making this determination, they must consider their own needs and those of their customers. The relevance of having an objective at any particular level or function is left to the organization to determine.

Once the policy is established, the organization must deploy it. This means it must be communicated to all involved in ways that are understandable. Understanding of the policy implies that everyone in the organization knows his or her role in carrying out the policy. This is much more than being able to quote what the policy says; everyone should clearly understand their roles in ensuring that the policy is implemented.

The policy must also be reviewed to ensure its continuing suitability. This review should be conducted at a time and in a manner that best suits the organization's needs. If goals and objectives are tightly tied to the policy, then the review can become an ongoing activity. In some organizations it might be more appropriate for the policy to be reviewed periodically as part of a strategic planning process or as part of management review. In any event, the policy should not be considered a static one but rather one that evolves as the organization, its customers, and its products change over time.

The objectives need not be included in the policy itself, but the policy must provide some basis for establishing and reviewing them.

 ISO 9001:1994 required that policy be relevant to the expectations and needs of customers. ISO 9001:2000 goes further by mandating commitment to meeting requirements. The requirements include those of the organization itself, any applicable regulatory requirements, and customer-specified requirements. Requirements also include those derived from customer expectations and needs that customers may not have directly stated or specified.

Some organizations have dynamic quality policies that actually include the objectives and numerical goals for overall organizational performance. Because the goals change from time to time, this type of policy must be updated often, which provides a clear opportunity to validate the objectives and commitment components of the policy.

Other organizations find the inclusion of objectives in the policy to be cumbersome. It is important for each organization to find a method of developing, deploying, and reviewing the quality policy that fits its needs.

The notes to the definition of quality policy in ISO 9000 provide some insight into policy development. These notes are informative, and thus they are not among the requirements.

Managers who want successful quality management systems should align the quality policy with the strategies and needs of their businesses. Organizations should consider the eight quality management principles stated in ISO 9000:2000 as a guide to policy development. These principles were input for developing the ISO 9000:2000 family of standards, but they are not requirements of ISO 9001:2000, and they should never be used as a basis for compliance audits to ISO 9001:2000.

DEFINITIONS

Quality policy (3.2.4)—overall intentions and direction of an **organization** (3.3.1) related to **quality** (3.1.1) as formally expressed by **top management** (3.2.7)

NOTE 1   Generally the quality policy is consistent with the overall policy of the organization and provides a framework for the setting of **quality objectives** (3.2.5).

NOTE 2   Quality management principles presented in this International Standard can form a basis for the establishment of a quality policy. (See 0.2.)

Requirement (3.1.2)—need or expectation that is stated, generally implied or obligatory

NOTE 1   "Generally implied" means that it is custom or common practice for the **organization** (3.3.1), its **customers** (3.3.5) and other **interested parties** (3.3.7), that the need or expectation under consideration is implied.

NOTE 2   A qualifier can be used to denote a specific type of requirement, e.g. product requirement, quality management requirement, customer requirement.

NOTE 3   A specified requirement is one which is stated, for example, in a **document** (3.7.2).

NOTE 4   Requirements can be generated by different interested parties.

Source: ANSI/ISO/ASQ Q9000-2000

 TYPICAL AUDIT ITEMS FOR COMPLIANCE

Items representing a difference from ISO 9001:1994 have a Δ at the end.

- Has a quality policy been developed?
- Does the quality policy include commitment to meeting requirements and commitment to continual improvement? Δ
- Does the quality policy provide a framework for establishing and reviewing the quality objectives? Δ
- Are quality objectives quantified? Δ
- Has top management determined that the quality policy meets the needs of the organization and its customers?
- Is the policy communicated to and understood by all in the organization?

- Are the members of the organization clear as to their role in carrying out the policy? Δ
- Is the quality policy included in the document control process? Δ
- Is the quality policy reviewed for continuing suitability? Δ

5.4 Planning

5.4.1 Quality objectives

Top management shall ensure that quality objectives, including those needed to meet requirements for product [see 7.1 a)], are established at relevant functions and levels within the organization. The quality objectives shall be measurable and consistent with the quality policy.

5.4.2 Quality management system planning

Top management shall ensure that

a) the planning of the quality management system is carried out in order to meet the requirements given in 4.1, as well as the quality objectives, and

b) the integrity of the quality management system is maintained when changes to the quality management system are planned and implemented.

Source: ANSI/ISO/ASQ Q9001-2000

The quantification of objectives implied in ISO 9001:1994 is now a specific requirement. Clause 5.4.1 requires that objectives be measurable. In many organizations, quality objectives are quantitative targets or goals. Where more abstract statements are used as quality objectives, organizations may need to review them to ensure they are measurable. Thus, objectives may be stated in any form suitable to the circumstances but eventually must be quantified so that performance can be measured. Many organizations find that quantifiable objectives are a useful tool in achieving conformity and continual improvement. The term *objective* is to be interpreted broadly to be the same as *goal, target,* or *aim.*

The organization must include the objectives needed to meet the requirements for products. To set such objectives, there must be an understanding of the processes that are important in meeting requirements. Key process outputs that are important to the customer must be identified, and the processes that create those outputs must be understood. This basic process information can be used as the first step in determining the important objectives. To determine lower-level objectives, *relevant* processes can then be broken down so that the key objectives can be defined at each organizational level and function. As the objectives flow through the levels and functions of the organization, they may take on different terms so that a number of lower-level objectives may be needed to support a higher-level objective.

There is also a requirement that the objectives be consistent with continual improvement of the effectiveness of the quality management system. Where output does not meet customer requirements, targeting quality management system improvements can lead to improved effectiveness in achieving an acceptable level of performance. Where output meets customer needs, the objectives may relate to maintaining or improving the system so that the customer requirements can be met more rapidly or with fewer in-process defects.

Once objectives have been set, the organization must identify and plan the resources needed to achieve them. The planning must determine and document the activities and associated resources required to meet objectives. This includes identification and planning of the quality management system processes and the interaction among those processes. Basic product-realization processes should be identified and understood in sufficient detail to plan the quality management system. Planning of product-realization processes is a separate concept and is covered in clause 7.1.

Planning must include considerations for meeting all of the requirements of clause 4.1, including the actions needed for continually improving the processes of the quality management system. This means that the measurement, analysis, and review processes needed for achieving the enhanced effectiveness of the quality management system must be identified and linked as a set of mutually supporting activities as stated in clauses 8.1 and 8.5.1.

Resource needs must be determined in accordance with clause 6.1, and this determination is best made by considering the processes necessary to operate and improve the quality management system. The quality management system should be effective in helping the organization to meet its objectives. For this reason, as the objectives are reviewed and changed over time, the quality management system must also evolve; it must be improved.

Clause 5.4.2 also requires management of change so that the integrity of the quality management system is maintained when the system is changed. Changes to the system can result from modifications to organizational structure, the introduction of new technology, turnover of personnel, or significant increases or decreases in volume. Change can also be driven by a need to improve the system's efficiency by eliminating activities perceived as non–value-adding. The organization should have a basic process to deal with these types of changes as they occur. The process should provide for addressing quality management system changes in a controlled manner. The details of the controls needed for implementing any specific change will require specific decisions at the time, but the basic process should be worked out as part of quality system planning. This process must include the identification of changes that could affect the quality management system as an input to management reviews.

The requirement for controlling change and maintaining the integrity of the quality management system as the system changes is new. Since we live in an era of constant change, this is a very important concept to understand. It is not intended that the requirements prevent change; rather, organizations must conduct change activities in a controlled manner that does not negatively affect the quality management system.

SERVICES

In the planning process, service organizations should consider the differences in setting objectives for the parts of the organization that provide service in direct contact with the customer. Objectives that relate to levels of service performance can sometimes be established between the organization and the customer. Defining the key processes that actually create the service for the customer can help in the determination of the objectives.

HARDWARE, SOFTWARE, AND PROCESSED MATERIALS

While the most important objectives may relate directly to the organization's hardware, software, or processed materials, there may be other aspects of the customers' needs (such as delivery timing, customer service, or price) that are equally important and should not be ignored in determining objectives.

 DEFINITIONS

Process (3.4.1)—set of interrelated or interacting activities which transforms inputs into outputs

NOTE 1   Inputs to a process are generally outputs of other processes.
NOTE 2   Processes in an **organization** (3.3.1) are generally planned and carried out under controlled conditions to add value.
NOTE 3   A process where the **conformity** (3.6.1) of the resulting **product** (3.4.2) cannot be readily or economically verified is frequently referred to as a "special process".

Quality objective (3.2.5)—something sought, or aimed for, related to **quality** (3.1.1)

NOTE 1   Quality objectives are generally based on the organization's **quality policy** (3.2.4).
NOTE 2   Quality objectives are generally specified for relevant functions and levels in the **organization** (3.3.1).

Quality planning (3.2.9)—part of **quality management** (3.2.8) focused on setting **quality objectives** (3.2.5) and specifying necessary operational **processes** (3.4.1) and related resources to fulfil the quality objectives

NOTE   Establishing **quality plans** (3.7.5) can be part of quality planning.

Source: ANSI/ISO/ASQ Q9000-2000

CONSIDERATIONS FOR DOCUMENTATION

ISO 9001:2000 does not require specific documented procedures for this clause. The requirements of clause 4.2.1, *General documentation requirements*, state that the organization must determine the documentation to "ensure the effective planning, operation and control of its processes." The quality manual or other documents should discuss how the planning activities take place and how planning is periodically updated. This clause does not require any specific quality records.

TYPICAL AUDIT ITEMS FOR COMPLIANCE

Items representing a difference from ISO 9001:1994 have a Δ at the end.

- Have quality objectives been established at each relevant function and level in the organization? Δ

- Do quality objectives include those needed to meet requirements for the organization's products or services?

- Has the organization identified the activities and processes required to meet objectives? Quality management system processes? Product or service-realization processes? Verification processes? Exclusions under clause 1.2? Δ

- Does quality planning include continual improvement of the processes of the quality management system? Δ

- Does quality planning take into account the needs of the organization as changes occur? Δ

5.5 Responsibility, authority and communication

5.5.1 Responsibility and authority

Top management shall ensure that responsibilities and authorities are defined and communicated within the organization.

5.5.2 Management representative

Top management shall appoint a member of management who, irrespective of other responsibilities, shall have responsibility and authority that includes

a) ensuring that processes needed for the quality management system are established, implemented and maintained,

b) reporting to top management on the performance of the quality management system and any need for improvement, and

c) ensuring the promotion of awareness of customer requirements throughout the organization.

NOTE   The responsibility of a management representative can include liaison with external parties on matters relating to the quality management system.

5.5.3 Internal communication

Top management shall ensure that appropriate communication processes are established within the organization and that communication takes place regarding the effectiveness of the quality management system.

Source: ANSI/ISO/ASQ Q9001-2000

The various roles of personnel in the organization must be defined so that their responsibility and authority, and interactions are clear. These roles must be communicated clearly to all in the organization who have a need to know them. This type of clarity is important for all key personnel involved with the quality management system. This was fundamental in ISO 9001:1994. ISO 9001:2000 goes further by requiring that these responsibilities and authorities be defined and communicated. Organization charts are often used to document and communicate the responsibility and authority of personnel.

It is especially important to make clear the authority and responsibilities of those in the organization who must identify nonconformities and require that corrective action be taken. This type of activity can involve anyone from senior managers to production workers, depending on the organization's size, complexity, and operating philosophy.

There is also a specific requirement that top management appoint a management representative. Management representatives must fulfill specific duties, including the following:

* They must ensure that the quality management system is implemented and maintained in accordance with ISO 9001. The representatives act as a link with top management and ensure that the system's status and improvement needs are communicated to top management. Normally it is the management representative who acts as the primary interface person with outside parties in relation to the quality management system. This often includes interaction with, for example, customer representatives or third-party auditing organizations.

* They must ensure that there is awareness of customer requirements throughout the organization. This means that there must be a process for communicating customer requirements. The management representative has flexibility in determining how to address this requirement.

Although adequate communication has always been a key to successful quality management system implementation, the requirement for internal communications is new with ISO 9001:2000. There must be adequate communications about the effectiveness of the system. These communications can take place in any manner that best suits the needs of the organization.

DEFINITIONS

Customer (3.3.5)—**organization** (3.3.1) or person that receives a **product** (3.4.2)

EXAMPLE   Consumer, client, end-user, retailer, beneficiary and purchaser.
NOTE   A customer can be internal or external to the organization.

Requirement (3.1.2)—need or expectation that is stated, generally implied or obligatory

NOTE 1   "Generally implied" means that it is custom or common practice for the **organization** (3.3.1), its **customers** (3.3.5) and other **interested parties** (3.3.7), that the need or expectation under consideration is implied.
NOTE 2   A qualifier can be used to denote a specific type of requirement, e.g. product requirement, quality management requirement, customer requirement.
NOTE 3   A specified requirement is one which is stated, for example, in a **document** (3.7.2).
NOTE 4   Requirements can be generated by different interested parties.

Top management (3.2.7)—person or group of people who directs and controls an **organization** (3.3.1) at the highest level

Source: ANSI/ISO/ASQ Q9000-2000

 TYPICAL AUDIT ITEMS FOR COMPLIANCE

Items representing a difference from ISO 9001:1994 have a Δ at the end.

- Are the organization's functions defined and communicated to facilitate effective quality management?
- Are responsibilities and authorities defined and communicated to facilitate effective quality management?
- Has top management appointed one or more management representatives as appropriate?
- Has top management defined the responsibilities and authority of the management representative?

- Does the management representative ensure that the processes of the quality management system are established and maintained? How?
- Does the management representative report to top management on the performance of the quality management system?
- Does the management representative promote awareness of customer requirements throughout the organization? Δ
- Do discussions with employees at all levels indicate that the organization effectively communicates processes of the quality management system and their effectiveness? Δ

5.6 Management review

5.6.1 General

Top management shall review the organization's quality management system, at planned intervals, to ensure its continuing suitability, adequacy and effectiveness. This review shall include assessing opportunities for improvement and the need for changes to the quality management system, including the quality policy and quality objectives.

Records from management reviews shall be maintained (see 4.2.4).

5.6.2 Review input

The input to management review shall include information on

a) results of audits,

b) customer feedback,

c) process performance and product conformity,

d) status of preventive and corrective actions,

e) follow-up actions from previous management reviews,

f) changes that could affect the quality management system, and

g) recommendations for improvement.

Source: ANSI/ISO/ASQ Q9001-2000

5.6.3 Review output

The output from the management review shall include any decisions and actions related to

a) improvement of the effectiveness of the quality management system and its processes,

b) improvement of product related to customer requirements, and

c) resource needs.

Source: ANSI/ISO/ASQ Q9001-2000

Management review of the quality system is the responsibility of top management. This is no different than the requirement of ISO 9001:1994. ISO 9001:1994 also required review at defined intervals of the continuing suitability and effectiveness of the system in meeting the standard, the organization's quality policy, and objectives.

ISO 9001:2000 contains additional requirements by specifying minimum review input items and output actions. The intent is generally the same as it was with ISO 9001:1994, and many organizations will have already structured a management review process that complies with the new requirements. But the wording of the new standard is much more prescriptive. Inputs for the reviews must now include customer feedback, process and product performance, status of preventive and corrective actions, changes that could affect the quality management system, and the results of audits. In addition, there is now a requirement to review follow-up actions from earlier management reviews.

Outputs of the management review are also specified and must include the following three types of actions:

- Management reviews must identify opportunities to improve the quality management system and its processes. These could include actions to simplify or foolproof processes, to develop improved methods, to improve documentation, and so on.

- "Improvement of product related to customer requirements . . ." This phrase is important—there is no requirement to improve the product beyond the point where all customer requirements are met. Improvements related to customer requirements could be items related to improved conformity with known requirements. On the other hand, remember that the top management is required in clause 5.2 to ". . . ensure that customer requirements are determined and met with the aim of enhancing customer satisfaction. . . ." It is important to recognize that these customer needs and expectations may change often so that organizations may also identify new customer requirements and establish actions to meet them.

- Actions related to resource needs, which would include ensuring that resources are provided as needed for continual operation and improvement of the quality management system.

 DEFINITIONS

Customer (3.3.5)—**organization** (3.3.1) or person that receives a **product** (3.4.2)

EXAMPLE   Consumer, client, end-user, retailer, beneficiary and purchaser.
NOTE   A customer can be internal or external to the organization.

Effectiveness (3.2.14)—extent to which planned activities are realized and planned results achieved

Product (3.4.2)—result of a **process** (3.4.1)

NOTE 1   There are four generic product categories, as follows:
—services (e.g. transport);
—software (e.g. computer program, dictionary);
—hardware (e.g. engine mechanical part);
—processed materials (e.g. lubricant).

Many products comprise elements belonging to different generic product categories. Whether the product is then called service, software, hardware or processed material depends on the dominant element. For example the offered product "automobile" consists of hardware (e.g. tyres), processed materials (e.g. fuel, cooling liquid), software (e.g. engine control software, driver's manual), and service (e.g. operating explanations given by the salesman).

NOTE 2   Service is the result of at least one activity necessarily performed at the interface between the **supplier** (3.3.6) and **customer** (3.3.5) and is generally intangible. Provision of a service can involve, for example, the following:

—an activity performed on a customer-supplied tangible product (e.g. automobile to be repaired);

—an activity performed on a customer-supplied intangible product (e.g. the income statement needed to prepare a tax return);

—the delivery of an intangible product (e.g. the delivery of information in the context of knowledge transmission);

—the creation of ambience for the customer (e.g. in hotels and restaurants).

Software consists of information and is generally intangible and can be in the form of approaches, transactions or **procedures** (3.4.5).

Hardware is generally tangible and its amount is a countable **characteristic** (3.5.1). Processed materials are generally tangible and their amount is a continuous characteristic. Hardware and processed materials often are referred to as goods.

NOTE 3   **Quality assurance** (3.2.11) is mainly focused on intended product

Requirement (3.1.2)—need or expectation that is stated, generally implied or obligatory

NOTE 1   "Generally implied" means that it is custom or common practice for the **organization** (3.3.1), its **customers** (3.3.5) and other **interested parties** (3.3.7), that the need or expectation under consideration is implied.

NOTE 2   A qualifier can be used to denote a specific type of requirement, e.g. product requirement, quality management requirement, customer requirement.

NOTE 3   A specified requirement is one which is stated, for example, in a **document** (3.7.2).

NOTE 4   Requirements can be generated by different interested parties.

Review (3.8.7)—activity undertaken to determine the suitability, adequacy and **effectiveness** (3.2.14) of the subject matter to achieve established objectives

NOTE   Review can also include the determination of **efficiency** (3.2.15).

EXAMPLE Management review, design and development review, review of customer requirements and nonconformity review.

Source: ANSI/ISO/ASQ Q9000-2000

TYPICAL AUDIT ITEMS FOR COMPLIANCE

Items representing a difference from ISO 9001:1994 have a Δ at the end.

- Does top management review the quality management system at planned intervals to ensure its continuing suitability, adequacy, and effectiveness?

- Do the management reviews include evaluation of the need for changes to the organization's quality management system, including quality policy and quality objectives?

- Does management review input include: results of audits, customer feedback, process performance, product conformity, status of preventive and corrective actions, follow-up actions from earlier management reviews, changes that could affect the quality management system, and recommendations for improvement? Δ

- Do the outputs of management reviews include actions related to the improvement of the quality management system and its processes? Δ

- Do the outputs of management reviews include actions related to the improvement of product related to customer requirements? Δ

- Do the outputs of management reviews include resource needs? Δ

- Are management review records maintained?

CHAPTER

4

Human and Other Resources

6 Resource management

6.1 Provision of resources

The organization shall determine and provide the resources needed

a) to implement and maintain the quality management system and continually improve its effectiveness, and

b) to enhance customer satisfaction by meeting customer requirements.

Source: ANSI/ISO/ASQ Q9001-2000

 The previous standard stated that resources needed to be available for generalized tasks: management, work, and verification activities, including internal audits. ISO 9001:2000 addresses resources that are needed for the entire quality management system—for implementation and improvement of the effectiveness of the quality management system and for enhancing customer satisfaction. This minimizes the misinterpretations that occurred previously. Organizations have always been expected to provide the resources needed to assure that product meets customer requirements. This is broader than just the quality function personnel or those people who do audits and inspections. The requirements have been made more clear about the extent of the resources that should be under consideration within this clause.

This clause covers all resources needed to meet the requirements of ISO 9001:2000. By defining the scope of this clause in these terms, the standard embraces the resource requirements of the entire quality management system.

The organization must identify what needs to be done to implement this standard. In determining the resource requirements, the organization should be specific to a level of detail that is appropriate. This usually includes detailing job responsibilities, authority, and interrelationships. Note that this is not a universal mandate. It may be an overwhelming bureaucratic burden for a small service organization to write out every job responsibility. For larger companies, however, effective operation requires the recording of job responsibilities and decision-making authority.

The term *resource* is often used in reference to personnel. In fact, this clause covers all resources needed to meet the requirements of the standard. Although the standard could never be specific as to what makes up these resources for each organization, normally this includes personnel, time, buildings, equipment, utilities, materials, supplies, instruments, software, and transport facilities.

The standard does not address the timeliness with which resources are to be provided. Timeliness was addressed in early drafts of ISO 9001 but was judged to be too subjective to be auditable. In any event, resources must be provided in a reasonable time frame. Just because a position has been defined or the need for a piece of equipment has been justified and approved for purchase does not mean that the organization has met its responsibilities. For example, jobs should not be left unfilled for indeterminate periods, and purchase orders should not be left open if there is a recognized need that has to be filled.

 DEFINITIONS

Customer satisfaction (3.1.4)—customer's perception of the degree to which the customer's **requirements** (3.1.2) have been fulfilled

NOTE 1   Customer complaints are a common indicator of low customer satisfaction but their absence does not necessarily imply high customer satisfaction.

NOTE 2   Even when customer requirements have been agreed with the customer and fulfilled, this does not necessarily ensure high customer satisfaction.

Process (3.4.1)—set of interrelated or interacting activities which transforms inputs into outputs

NOTE 1   Inputs to a process are generally outputs of other processes.

NOTE 2   Processes in an **organization** (3.3.1) are generally planned and carried out under controlled conditions to add value.

NOTE 3   A process where the **conformity** (3.6.1) of the resulting **product** (3.4.2) cannot be readily or economically verified is frequently referred to as a "special process".

Quality management system (3.2.3)—**management system** (3.2.2) to direct and control an **organization** (3.3.1) with regard to **quality** (3.1.1)

Source: ANSI/ISO/ASQ Q9000-2000

CONSIDERATIONS FOR DOCUMENTATION

The records that are created by the activities to meet the requirements of this clause may need to be controlled per clause 4.2.4, *Control of records*. The organization determines, in this case, whether records need to be controlled.

TYPICAL AUDIT ITEMS FOR COMPLIANCE

Items representing a difference from ISO 9001:1994 have a Δ at the end.

- Has the organization determined the resources necessary to implement the quality management system?
- Has the organization provided the resources necessary to implement the quality management system?
- Has the organization determined the resources necessary to improve the effectivness of the quality management system? Δ
- Has the organization provided the resources necessary to improve the effectiveness of the quality management system? Δ
- Has the organization determined the resources necessary to meet customer requirements?
- Has the organization determined the resources necessary to enhance customer satisfaction? Δ
- Has the organizational provided the resources necessary to enhance customer satisfaction? Δ

6.2 Human resources

6.2.1 General

Personnel performing work affecting product quality shall be competent on the basis of appropriate education, training, skills and experience.

Source: ANSI/ISO/ASQ Q9001-2000

The requirements of the 1994 standard have been clarified. Only parts of the requirements in ISO 9001:1994, clause 4.1.2.1, *Responsibility and authority,* and of clause 4.18, *Training,* can be found here. The remaining requirements of these clauses are contained in other clauses of this standard.

The intent of the 1994 standard, with the detailed listing of tasks in clause 4.1.2.1 and clause 4.1.2.2, was to include the personnel directly involved in managing product-related activities, performance of product-related work, and in product-related verification activities. ISO 9001:2000 includes all personnel that perform any work that affects product quality. This new wording has the same intent. Similar to the scope of the preceding clause on the provision of resources, the ISO 9001:2000 requirement is intended to encompass all personnel performing work that affects quality. Rather than trying to list all of these separate tasks as was done in 1994—a listing that experience has shown to be incomplete and open to misunderstanding—this clause contains a broad requirement that includes all of these personnel.

Clarity is also added with respect to personnel competency. ISO 9001:1994, clause 4.18, *Training,* explicitly required personnel assigned specific tasks to be qualified. Additional requirements for trained, qualified, and experienced personnel were scattered throughout the 1994 standard in various clauses, including clauses for quality systems, process control, and design and development planning. This requirement is now expressed succinctly in clause 6.

Written job requirements are usually needed in order to properly assign personnel. The requirement in clause 6.2.1 is that personnel are competent. Before the competency of employees can be assured, the organization needs to identify job requirements.

Although the quality management system extends throughout an organization, this clause does not include all personnel—even though, in principle, everyone's work affects the quality of the products supplied by the organization. With the quality management system now structured in four main clauses, it is now clear that the intent of the standard is to relate this requirement to the personnel "performing work affecting product quality." This clause includes personnel involved in top management, resource management, product realization, and measurement-analysis-improvement processes. All of these personnel are required to be competent based on education, training, skills, and experience.

 ## DEFINITIONS

Competence (3.9.12)—demonstrated ability to apply knowledge and skills

Quality management system (3.2.3)—**management system** (3.2.2) to direct and control an **organization** (3.3.1) with regard to **quality** (3.1.1)

Source: ANSI/ISO/ASQ Q9000-2000

 ## CONSIDERATIONS FOR DOCUMENTATION

The records that are created by the activities to assure competency may need to be controlled per clause 4.2.4, *Control of records.* In this case, the organization determines whether records need to be controlled.

TYPICAL AUDIT ITEMS FOR COMPLIANCE

- Are personnel who perform work affecting product quality competent based on education, training, skills, and experience?

6.2.2 Competence, awareness and training

The organization shall

a) determine the necessary competence for personnel performing work affecting product quality,

b) provide training or take other actions to satisfy these needs,

c) evaluate the effectiveness of the actions taken,

d) ensure that its personnel are aware of the relevance and importance of their activities and how they contribute to the achievement of the quality objectives, and

e) maintain appropriate records of education, training, skills and experience (see 4.2.4).

Source: ANSI/ISO/ASQ Q9001-2000

    This clause can be compared to ISO 9001:1994, clause 4.18, *Training.* There are new requirements, including the determination of needed competencies, a greater emphasis on taking whatever action is needed to close competency gaps, and a requirement to evaluate the effectiveness of the actions taken to close competency gaps. There is also a new requirement to ensure that employees are aware of the importance of their work.

The concept of determining competencies required and closing identified competency gaps is new. While training is mentioned as a primary means of accomplishing this, the new standard recognizes that there are other possibilities.

For example, organizations may hire new employees who have the needed competencies.

Having competent people is essential for the achievement of organizational objectives. This clause pertains to all personnel at all levels within the scope of this standard. It addresses all training and other actions needed to ensure competency for accomplishing assigned tasks.

 The organization must identify what classroom training, seminars, on-the-job, or other training is necessary so that every employee involved in the quality management system is competent. This is not the same thing as determining job requirements. Competency may be determined by comparisons between the job requirements that define what employees must do and the qualifications of the employee. Where training is needed, it must be provided. The training process should address the competency needs of employees so that they either can become competent or can stay competent.

 The training should include provisions to establish and maintain employee awareness of the importance of their work and how they contribute to the quality objectives of the organization. This training should be specific so that it relates to the responsibilities of each employee.

Evaluation of the effectiveness of the actions (including training) that are taken to close competency gaps is a new requirement. It is common practice to conduct training evaluations in the following three parts:

- Evaluation of the training immediately upon completion
- Evaluation of the training received several weeks after the training
- Evaluation of the skills developed several months after the training

One approach is to have the student's supervisor evaluate the work performance related to the training, both short term and over several months. This provides input for evaluating the adequacy of the training. If means other than training are used to close competency gaps, the effectiveness of these other actions must be evaluated as well. For example, if new personnel are hired, their performance could be evaluated periodically during the early stages of their employment.

DEFINITIONS

Quality (3.1.1)—degree to which a set of inherent **characteristics** (3.5.1) fulfils **requirements** (3.1.2)

NOTE 1   The term "quality" can be used with adjectives such as poor, good or excellent.
NOTE 2   "Inherent", as opposed to "assigned", means existing in something, especially as a permanent characteristic.

Effectiveness (3.2.14)—extent to which planned activities are realized and planned results achieved

Quality objective (3.2.5)—something sought, or aimed for, related to **quality** (3.1.1)

NOTE 1   Quality objectives are generally based on the organization's **quality policy** (3.2.4).
NOTE 2   Quality objectives are generally specified for relevant functions and levels in the **organization** (3.3.1).

Source: ANSI/ISO/ASQ Q9000-2000

CONSIDERATIONS FOR DOCUMENTATION

Often organizations will document a formal, annual training plan to address the training needs of personnel. The records dealing with personnel education, experience, training, and qualifications that are created by the activities to meet the requirements of this clause need to be controlled per clause 4.2.4, *Control of records.*

TYPICAL AUDIT ITEMS FOR COMPLIANCE

Items representing a difference from ISO 9001:1994 have a Δ at the end.

- Does the organization identify the competency needs of the individual personnel performing activities affecting quality, including additional training needs? Δ
- Does the organization provide training or take other actions to satisfy these needs? Δ
- Does the organization evaluate the effectiveness of the training provided or of other actions taken to ensure competency? Δ
- Does the organization ensure that employees are aware of the relevance and importance of their activities and how they contribute to the achievement of the quality objectives? Δ
- Does the organization maintain records of education, experience, training, and qualifications?

6.3 Infrastructure

The organization shall determine, provide and maintain the infrastructure needed to achieve conformity to product requirements. Infrastructure includes, as applicable

a) buildings, workspace and associated utilities,

b) process equipment (both hardware and software), and

c) supporting services (such as transport or communication).

Source: ANSI/ISO/ASQ Q9001-2000

There is now a clear statement that facilities and associated infrastructure elements are within the domain of this standard. Although ISO 9001:1994 does not explicitly state requirements for facilities and workspace, it has been widely understood that these were at least partially addressed in ISO 9001:1994, clause 4.9, *Control of processes,* which does require "suitable production, installation and servicing equipment." Sector-specific standards that contain additional requirements detail these additional facility requirements under clause 4.9. Common sense dictates that physical resources need to be provided for achieving the product. Quality management system records should indicate that the requirements of this clause have been considered and addressed.

This clause encompasses all of the physical resources needed to create the product and to provide it to the customer, except personnel. The requirements for personnel are covered in the preceding clause on human resources. Included in this clause are requirements to identify, provide, and maintain the infrastructure needed to achieve conformity of product. *Infrastructure* is broadly defined to encompass the buildings, workspace, equipment, and support services.

Infrastructure is one of the clauses under resource management. The significance of separating it from the old process control clause should be recognized. The organization must identify, provide, and maintain appropriate infrastructure for all of the processes within the quality management system. This goes beyond production and service operations and beyond even the realization processes to include the management processes; other resource processes (training, in particular); and the measurement, analysis, and improvement processes.

SERVICES

The availability of appropriate physical resources is equally important in the service sector. For a warehousing organization, successful performance is highly dependent on the availability of warehouses in the right location and with the right capabilities. Does the warehouse require air conditioning, for example? For a delivery service, the availability of delivery vehicles is critical. For a repair facility, appropriate diagnostic and repair instruments are needed. For a food service, appropriate kitchens, handling equipment, and vehicles are needed. In each case, successful service realization requires the appropriate identification, provision, and maintenance of physical resources.

HARDWARE, PROCESSED MATERIALS, AND SOFTWARE

Physical resources provide the foundation for the work that is required to implement the quality management system. Design and development of new software requires appropriate workrooms, appropriate programming tools, and appropriate processors. Manufacturing computer chips requires special clean rooms. Sterilizing medical devices requires special equipment and equipment controls. Special transports are required for the delivery of products such as fuel, oil, or milk. This new clause adds clarity of focus for a critical area that previously was assumed to be so obvious that it did not need to be identified as a unique requirement of the quality system.

 DEFINITIONS

Conformity (3.6.1)—fulfilment of a **requirement** (3.1.2)

NOTE 1   This definition is consistent with ISO/IEC Guide 2 but differs from it in phrasing to fit into the ISO 9000 concepts.
NOTE 2   The term "conformance" is synonymous but deprecated.

Infrastructure (3.3.3)—system of facilities, equipment and services needed for the operation of an **organization** (3.3.1)

Source: ANSI/ISO/ASQ Q9000-2000

 CONSIDERATIONS FOR DOCUMENTATION

The records that are created by the activities to meet the requirements of this clause may need to be controlled per clause 4.2.4, *Control of records*. In this case, the organization determines whether records need to be controlled.

 TYPICAL AUDIT ITEMS FOR COMPLIANCE

- Does the organization identify, provide, and maintain the workspace and associated facilities it needs to achieve the conformity of product?

- Does the organization identify, provide, and maintain the equipment, hardware, and software it needs to achieve the conformity of product?

- Does the organization identify, provide, and maintain the supporting services it needs to achieve the conformity of product?

6.4 Work environment

The organization shall determine and manage the work environment needed to achieve conformity to product requirements.

Source: ANSI/ISO/ASQ Q9001-2000

Clause 6.4 is not a new requirement. The requirement that "a suitable working environment" be provided is contained in ISO 9001:1994, clause 4.9, *Process control.* Including the requirement for work environment in the resource management clause applies this concept to all of the processes of the quality management system needed to achieve conformity of product. This is a broader application than in 1994.

The work environment of an organization can be considered to be a combination of human and physical factors. Examples of human factors in the work environment that may affect conformity of product include the following:

- Work methods
- Safety rules and guidance, including use of protective equipment
- Ergonomics

Physical factors can also affect the ability to achieve conforming product. It is important to control those factors that affect product quality characteristics, since they have a direct impact on the ability of the product to conform to specifications.

Examples of physical factors affecting the work environment may include the following:

- Heat
- Hygiene
- Vibration
- Noise
- Humidity
- Pollution
- Light
- Cleanliness
- Air flow

If the organization determines that it is necessary to control work areas for physical factors, it is common to consider the following:

- Identify standards to be maintained.
- Assure that the facility meets the standards.
- Train personnel on standards pertaining to their work.
- Prohibit unauthorized access to the work area.
- Implement and maintain desired physical conditions.
- Maintain records of the conditions as a means of demonstrating compliance to the standards.

SERVICES

Good personal hygiene of food service and pharmacy employees, for example, is important to prevent the contamination of customer product. Such factors are often tightly controlled by regulatory standards.

HARDWARE AND PROCESSED MATERIALS

Physical factors of the work environment include factors such as ambient humidity and temperature in a paint shop. Control of these factors is necessary to obtain a conforming painted surface. To achieve high performance of electronic components, particle contamination needs to be kept extremely low during fabrication.

DEFINITIONS

Work environment (3.3.4)—set of conditions under which work is performed

NOTE Conditions include physical, social, psychological and environmental factors (such as temperature, recognition schemes, ergonomics and atmospheric composition).

Conformity (3.6.1)—fulfilment of a **requirement** (3.1.2)

NOTE 1   This definition is consistent with ISO/IEC Guide 2 but differs from it in phrasing to fit into the ISO 9000 concepts.

NOTE 2   The term "conformance" is synonymous but deprecated.

Source: ANSI/ISO/ASQ Q9000-2000

CONSIDERATIONS FOR DOCUMENTATION

The records that are created by the activities to meet the requirements of this clause may need to be controlled per clause 4.2.4, *Control of records*. In this case, the organization determines whether records need to be controlled.

TYPICAL AUDIT ITEMS FOR COMPLIANCE

- Does the organization identify the conditions in the work environment that must be controlled to achieve conformity of product?

- Does the organization manage the human and physical factors of the work environment needed to achieve conformity of product?

CHAPTER

5

Planning of Product Realization and Customer-Related Processes

7 Product realization

7.1 Planning of product realization

The organization shall plan and develop the processes needed for product realization. Planning of product realization shall be consistent with the requirements of the other processes of the quality management system (see 4.1).

In planning product realization, the organization shall determine the following, as appropriate:

a) quality objectives and requirements for the product;

b) the need to establish processes, documents, and provide resources specific to the product;

c) required verification, validation, monitoring, inspection and test activities specific to the product and the criteria for product acceptance;

d) records needed to provide evidence that the realization processes and resulting product meet requirements (see 4.2.4).

The output of this planning shall be in a form suitable for the organization's method of operations.

NOTE 1   A document specifying the processes of the quality management system (including the product realization processes) and the resources to be applied to a specific product, project or contract, can be referred to as a quality plan.

NOTE 2   The organization may also apply the requirements given in 7.3 to the development of product realization processes.

Source: ANSI/ISO/ASQ Q9001-2000

Much of the content of clause 7.1 was developed from various clauses of ISO 9001:1994 (for example, clauses 4.2.3, 4.9, 4.10, 4.12, 4.15, and 4.19). The requirements were generally defined more narrowly in 1994, except for the sweeping requirement in clause 4.9 that required processes that directly affect quality to be carried out under controlled conditions. Although clause 7.1 consists of only three short paragraphs, it is one of the most important clauses in ISO 9001:2000. Along with clause 4.1 and clause 8.1, clause 7.1

provides the essence of the use of the process approach. It requires organizations to *think* about and plan all of the processes that, when linked together, will result in the delivery of products that will conform to customer requirements, create customer satisfaction, and foster continual improvement. The planning of realization processes also must be consistent with the other requirements of the quality management system and must be documented in a form that is appropriate for the organization.

The planning activity required by clause 7.1 may not be a trivial exercise. Fewer documented procedures may be required than in the past, and no specific format is dictated, but ISO 9001:2000 demands that the organization understand the processes needed to deliver conforming products to customers. These processes must be understood not only with respect to the products themselves but also in the broader context of the objectives of the organization and any other requirements of the quality management system. The planning activity for realization processes must address the quality objectives and requirements for the product; the need to establish appropriate processes and documentation; the need to provide resources and facilities specific to the product; required verification, validation, monitoring, inspection, and test activities; and the criteria for acceptability of the product. The organization is also required to determine what records are necessary to provide confidence that the processes and resulting product conform to requirements.

Many organizations will have little trouble conforming to these requirements, since processes and documentation already exist to address them. For others, this will require some careful thought. Perhaps flowcharts or process mapping will be appropriate to assure that all process steps are addressed in terms of the availability of documentation, facilities, personnel, and any other required resources.

The 1994 standard mentioned quality plans as one approach to quality planning for products. In note 1 to this clause, a product quality plan is described, the implication being that a quality plan can be one way to document the quality planning for a product.

There is also a note 2, which offers the advice that an organization should consider using the same planning approach when designing product realization processes as it uses to design new hardware or service products. From the viewpoint of operating effectiveness, it is strongly suggested that organizations control the design of their realization processes with the same rigor that they dedicate to products, even though this is not a specific requirement of ISO 9001.

 DEFINITIONS

Requirement (3.1.2)—need or expectation that is stated, generally implied or obligatory

NOTE 1   "Generally implied" means that it is custom or common practice for the **organization** (3.3.1), its **customers** (3.3.5) and other **interested parties** (3.3.7), that the need or expectation under consideration is implied.

NOTE 2   A qualifier can be used to denote a specific type of requirement, e.g. product requirement, quality management requirement, customer requirement.

NOTE 3   A specified requirement is one which is stated, for example, in a **document** (3.7.2).

NOTE 4   Requirements can be generated by different interested parties.

Capability (3.1.5)—ability of an **organization** (3.3.1), **system** (3.2.1) or **process** (3.4.1) to realize a **product** (3.4.2) that will fulfil the **requirements** (3.1.2) for that product

NOTE   Process capability terms in the field of statistics are defined in ISO 3534-2.

Quality planning (3.2.9)—part of **quality management** (3.2.8) focused on setting **quality objectives** (3.2.5) and specifying necessary operational **processes** (3.4.1) and related resources to fulfil the quality objectives

NOTE   Establishing **quality plans** (3.7.5) can be part of quality planning.

Process (3.4.1)—set of interrelated or interacting activities which transforms inputs into outputs

NOTE 1   Inputs to a process are generally outputs of other processes.

NOTE 2   Processes in an **organization** (3.3.1) are generally planned and carried out under controlled conditions to add value.

NOTE 3   A process where the **conformity** (3.6.1) of the resulting **product** (3.4.2) cannot be readily or economically verified is frequently referred to as a "special process".

Product (3.4.2)—result of a **process** (3.4.1)

NOTE 1   There are four generic product categories, as follows:

—services (e.g. transport);

—software (e.g. computer program, dictionary);

—hardware (e.g. engine mechanical part);

—processed materials (e.g. lubricant).

Many products comprise elements belonging to different generic product categories. Whether the product is then called service, software, hardware or processed material depends on the dominant element. For example the offered product "automobile" consists of hardware (e.g. tyres), processed materials (e.g. fuel, cooling liquid), software (e.g. engine control software, driver's manual), and service (e.g. operating explanations given by the salesman).

NOTE 2   Service is the result of at least one activity necessarily performed at the interface between the **supplier** (3.3.6) and **customer** (3.3.5) and is generally intangible. Provision of a service can involve, for example, the following:

—an activity performed on a customer-supplied tangible product (e.g. automobile to be repaired);

—an activity performed on a customer-supplied intangible product (e.g. the income statement needed to prepare a tax return);

—the delivery of an intangible product (e.g. the delivery of information in the context of knowledge transmission);

—the creation of ambience for the customer (e.g. in hotels and restaurants).

Software consists of information and is generally intangible and can be in the form of approaches, transactions or **procedures** (3.4.5).

Hardware is generally tangible and its amount is a countable **characteristic** (3.5.1). Processed materials are generally tangible and their amount is a continuous characteristic. Hardware and processed materials often are referred to as goods.

NOTE 3   **Quality assurance** (3.2.11) is mainly focused on intended product.

Source: ANSI/ISO/ASQ Q9000-2000

CONSIDERATIONS FOR DOCUMENTATION

The organization should consider preparing a documented procedure to describe how the planning is accomplished. Alternatively, the planning of product realization could be described in the quality manual. Where a documented procedure is developed, it is recommended that standard checklists and other planning formats be developed and incorporated into the document. This clause also has a specific requirement that the planning define the records required to provide confidence of conformity to requirements.

 TYPICAL AUDIT ITEMS FOR COMPLIANCE

Items representing a difference from ISO 9001:1994 have a Δ at the end.

- Is there evidence of planning of production processes?
- Does the planning extend beyond production processes to encompass all product realization processes? Δ
- Is the planning consistent with other elements of the quality management system? Δ
- Does product realization documentation exist?
- Are product realization resources and facilities defined during the planning process, and do they appear to be adequate?
- Does the planning define the records that must be prepared to provide confidence in the conformity of the processes and resulting product?

7.2 Customer-related process

7.2.1 Determination of requirements related to the product

The organization shall determine

a) requirements specified by the customer, including the requirements for delivery and post-delivery activities,

b) requirements not stated by the customer but necessary for specified or intended use, where known,

c) statutory and regulatory requirements related to the product, and

d) any additional requirements determined by the organization.

Source: ANSI/ISO/ASQ Q9001-2000

How important to an organization is the process of determining customer requirements? It is so important that it demands attention as a survival issue by every part of the organization. The quotation and order process has an enormous impact on ultimate customer satisfaction; if customer requirements are not bilaterally understood, the probability of achieving ultimate customer satisfaction is seriously diminished. Therefore, it is a business necessity to have an effective process established and implemented to identify customerrequirements.

Compliance is not difficult for organizations providing off-the-shelf catalog products manufactured to published specifications or standardized services with normal delivery requirements. However, if customers are purchasing complex systems with custom engineering and software according to a complex set of commercial terms, it is essential to obtain a clear understanding of customer requirements by whatever means possible, including activities such as holding face-to-face meetings and attending pre-bid meetings.

Most of the concepts in this clause were implied in ISO 9001:1994 (clause 4.3, *Contract review*), but there is now a specific requirement for the organization to address product requirements that have not been specified by the customer but are necessary for the intended or specified use of the product.

Full determination of customer requirements is often an iterative process. Often there are known issues that may evolve into real requirements at a later stage. In such cases, documentation of the open issues and providing for the attendant business risk may prove to be an acceptable approach to meeting the requirements of this clause.

 DEFINITIONS

Customer (3.3.5)—**organization** (3.3.1) or person that receives a **product** (3.4.2)

EXAMPLE   Consumer, client, end-user, retailer, beneficiary and purchaser.
NOTE   A customer can be internal or external to the organization.

Requirement (3.1.2)—need or expectation that is stated, generally implied or obligatory

NOTE 1   "Generally implied" means that it is custom or common practice for the **organization** (3.3.1), its **customers** (3.3.5) and other **interested parties** (3.3.7), that the need or expectation under consideration is implied.

NOTE 2   A qualifier can be used to denote a specific type of requirement, e.g. product requirement, quality management requirement, customer requirement.

NOTE 3   A specified requirement is one which is stated, for example, in a **document** (3.7.2).

NOTE 4   Requirements can be generated by different interested parties.

Source: ANSI/ISO/ASQ Q9000-2000

CONSIDERATIONS FOR DOCUMENTATION

The determination of customer requirements is a critical activity and generally involves several functions and levels in an organization. It is wise to have a documented procedure to determine all aspects of customer requirements. The documented procedure should include determining product requirements specified by the customer and product requirements not specified by the customer but necessary for intended or specified use. Also, unique regulatory and statutory requirements should be considered. This procedure could be included in a broader document addressing customer communications (see clause 7.2.3).

Clause 7.2.1 also does not require any specific records. The planning for realization processes covered in clause 7.1 should define the records the organization will keep during the process of determining customer requirements. Organizations should consider keeping records of the written requirements and any documentation of conversations in which orally transmitted requirements are discussed.

TYPICAL AUDIT ITEMS FOR COMPLIANCE

Items representing a difference from ISO 9001:1994 have a Δ at the end.

- Does the organization determine customer requirements?
- Does the process include the determination of requirements needed but not specified? Δ
- Are records available that provide evidence that customer requirements have been determined?

7.2.2 Review of requirements related to the product

The organization shall review the requirements related to the product. This review shall be conducted prior to the organization's commitment to supply a product to the customer (e.g. submission of tenders, acceptance of contracts or orders, acceptance of changes to contracts or orders) and shall ensure that

a) product requirements are defined,

b) contract or order requirements differing from those previously expressed are resolved, and

c) the organization has the ability to meet the defined requirements.

Records of the results of the review and actions arising from the review shall be maintained (see 4.2.4).

Where the customer provides no documented statement of requirement, the customer requirements shall be confirmed by the organization before acceptance.

Where product requirements are changed, the organization shall ensure that relevant documents are amended and that relevant personnel are made aware of the changed requirements.

NOTE   In some situations, such as internet sales, a formal review is impractical for each order. Instead the review can cover relevant product information such as catalogues or advertising material.

Source: ANSI/ISO/ASQ Q9001-2000

Like clause 7.2.1, this clause applies to all product types, to all market sectors, and to organizations of all sizes. This clause contains similar requirements to clause 4.3.2 in ISO 9001:1994.

The acceptance of an order or the submission of a quote or a tender by an organization creates an obligation on the organization to meet the conditions stated in the order or to provide the goods and services included in the scope of the quotation or tender. The obligation assumed by the organization includes not only the products defined but also ancillary items such as conformance to stated delivery dates, adherence to referenced external standards, and compliance with the commercial terms and conditions applicable to the order, contract, quote, or tender.

The complexity of the order/quote review process depends on the business of the organization. A process for reviewing verbal orders for off-the-shelf products with 24-hour delivery (for example, software packages) will differ considerably from a process for reviewing a large order for a one-of-a-kind product with a two-year delivery (for example, an order for a control system for an electric power generating station). The review process must also accommodate, as applicable, electronic orders, blanket orders with periodic releases, unsolicited orders, orders through distributors or representatives, faxed orders, and an almost infinite combination of these and other possibilities. The note to this clause, for example, recognizes that Internet transactions will require creative thinking on the part of organizations to efficiently review customer requirements.

With such a spectrum of possibilities, what is an organization expected to do to conform to the requirements? The first step should be to develop a clear understanding of the nature of the various kinds of customer requirements. If, for example, an organization publishes a catalog and accepts only written orders for catalog-listed items to standard delivery times, then a quotation and order or contract-review procedure can be as simple as a one-paragraph statement that a designated individual (for example, a manager, a clerk, or a president) shall review the written order and initial and date the order, indicating that its requirements can be met. If an organization must address possibilities that only occur rarely, the organization could simply note in a procedure that any circumstances different from standard terms and conditions will be addressed via a specific quality plan—which can be generated as the unique occasions arise.

Thus, for a simple order-entry process, there can be a very simple, brief, and effective contract-review process. For the large, complex contracts or quotations, the review process may involve many organizational entities such as engineering, manufacturing, legal, finance, and quality assurance. Accordingly, the procedures governing such reviews can be complex and lengthy.

A good guideline to keep in mind when developing a process to address the specific requirements of clause 7.2.2 is to balance the risks to the organization with the effort expended in a review of customer requirements, keeping in mind that the purpose of the review is to add value and not to create a bureaucratic morass.

Clause 7.2.2c requires that the organization have the ability to meet requirements. Often with advanced products there is a need to advance the state of the art as product development progresses. Such situations should be clearly identified so that the business risks are understood. In such cases, the defined requirement could be the development of the needed technological advance.

When changes to product requirements, orders, contracts, or quotations occur, it is a requirement that the organization assure that relevant documentation is amended and communicated, as appropriate, within the organization.

 ## CONSIDERATIONS FOR DOCUMENTATION

Organizations should consider documenting a process for the review of customer requirements and how these requirements can be met, as well as the consideration of additional requirements that may be appropriate.

This clause has a specific requirement for records that is self-explanatory—keep adequate records of reviews. It is worthwhile to establish minimum retention times for review documents (for example, three years or seven years). Some organizations have a cultural bias to retain such documents forever; however, it is usually not a good idea to create such a requirement by procedure unless required by a contract.

 ## TYPICAL AUDIT ITEMS FOR COMPLIANCE

• Does a process exist to require the review of identified customer requirements before commitment to supply a product to the customer?

- Does a process exist to require the review of quotes and orders to ensure that requirements are adequately defined?
- Is there a process for handling the review of verbal orders?
- Is there a process to handle the resolution of differences between quotations and orders?
- Does a process exist for handling changes to product requirements?
- Are records maintained of the results of reviews and actions taken?

7.2.3 Customer communication

The organization shall determine and implement effective arrangements for communicating with customers in relation to

a) product information,

b) enquiries, contracts or order handling, including amendments, and

c) customer feedback, including customer complaints.

Source: ANSI/ISO/ASQ Q9001-2000

 The basic requirements of this clause are not new. Customer communication has always been a requirement. However, the requirements for implementing arrangements with customers for communication on issues such as general feedback or specific complaints are broader in scope and more explicit than the requirements contained in ISO 9001:1994.

The arrangements identified and implemented should be appropriate for the organization in terms of its products, its orders or contracts, and the approaches to be used to obtain customer feedback.

CONSIDERATIONS FOR DOCUMENTATION

Determination of customer requirements is a critical activity and generally involves several functions and levels in an organization. Organizations should consider having a process to assure adequate communications with customers relating to product information, inquiries, contracts, order handling (including amendments), and customer feedback, including customer complaints. The extent to which the process should be documented will depend upon the size of the organization and the variety of customer communication links.

 TYPICAL AUDIT ITEMS FOR COMPLIANCE

Are there effective processes in place to communicate with customers about product information, inquiries, contracts, order handling (including amendments), and customer feedback, including customer complaints?

CHAPTER

6

Design and Development

7.3 Design and development

7.3.1 Design and development planning

The organization shall plan and control the design and development of product.

During the design and development planning, the organization shall determine

a) the design and development stages,

b) the review, verification and validation that are appropriate to each design and development stage, and

c) the responsibilities and authorities for design and development.

The organization shall manage the interfaces between different groups involved in design and development to ensure effective communication and clear assignment of responsibility.

Planning output shall be updated, as appropriate, as the design and development progresses.

Source: ANSI/ISO/ASQ Q9001-2000

The intent of clause 7.3.1 is to make sure that the organization plans and controls design and development projects. The key reason for this emphasis on planning is to maximize the probability that the project will meet defined requirements. If the design and development processes are planned and controlled well, an additional benefit should be that projects will be completed on time and within budget.

Planning is required to the level of detail needed to achieve the design and development objectives—not to generate an excessive amount of paperwork. A typical approach is to generate some form of project flowchart that incorporates the pertinent personnel, timing, and interrelationship information. Examples include Gantt charts, PERT charts, or CPM charts. The important effort is the thinking and discussion required to determine how the project will proceed from inception to completion. Stages of the project need to be determined, and responsibilities, authority, and interfaces need to be defined. Requirements need to be established for the incorporation of review, verification, and validation into the design and development project. The organization needs to determine how communications will be structured (for example, weekly meetings, periodic reports, or other methods). Widely available software can be a useful tool in meeting the planning requirements of the standard.

 DEFINITIONS

Design and development (3.4.4)—set of **processes** (3.4.1) that transforms **requirements** (3.1.2) into specified **characteristics** (3.5.1) or into the **specification** (3.7.3) of a **product** (3.4.2), **process** (3.4.1) or **system** (3.2.1)

NOTE 1   The terms "design" and "development" are sometimes used synonymously and sometimes used to define different stages of the overall design and development process.

NOTE 2   A qualifier can be applied to indicate the nature of what is being designed and developed (e.g. product design and development or process design and development).

Process (3.4.1)—set of interrelated or interacting activities which transforms inputs into outputs

NOTE 1   Inputs to a process are generally outputs of other processes.

NOTE 2   Processes in an **organization** (3.3.1) are generally planned and carried out under controlled conditions to add value.

NOTE 3   A process where the **conformity** (3.6.1) of the resulting **product** (3.4.2) cannot be readily or economically verified is frequently referred to as a "special process".

Project (3.4.3)—unique **process** (3.4.1), consisting of a set of coordinated and controlled activities with start and finish dates, undertaken to achieve an objective conforming to specific **requirements** (3.1.2), including the constraints of time, cost and resources

NOTE 1   An individual project can form part of a larger project structure.

NOTE 2   In some projects the objectives are refined and the product **characteristics** (3.5.1) defined progressively as the project proceeds.

NOTE 3   The outcome of a project may be one or several units of **product** (3.4.2).

NOTE 4   Adapted from ISO 10006:1997.

Characteristic (3.5.1)—distinguishing feature

NOTE 1   A characteristic can be inherent or assigned.
NOTE 2   A characteristic can be qualitative or quantitative.
NOTE 3   There are various classes of characteristic, such as the following:
—physical (e.g. mechanical, electrical, chemical or biological characteristics);
—sensory (e.g. related to smell, touch, taste, sight, hearing);
—behavioral (e.g. courtesy, honesty, veracity);
—temporal (e.g. punctuality, reliability, availability);
—ergonomic (e.g. physiological characteristic, or related to human safety);
—functional (e.g. maximum speed of an aircraft).

System (3.2.1)—set of interrelated or interacting elements

Source: ANSI/ISO/ASQ Q9000-2000

CONSIDERATIONS FOR DOCUMENTATION

Considerations should include a documented procedure that states the expectations for formal project plans, including the minimum level of detail for each project. The planning and documentation requirements are often a function of the size of the project. Note that the clause requires that the planning be updated as the project progresses. This clause also does not require any specific records. Organizations should determine which design and development planning records should be retained.

TYPICAL AUDIT ITEMS FOR COMPLIANCE

- Are the stages of the design and development project defined? Where? Δ
- Are verification and validation addressed? Are these activities appropriate?
- Is it clear who is responsible for what?
- Are the communications channels and interfaces defined and managed? Is there evidence that communication on projects is occurring and that it is effective?

7.3.2 Design and development inputs

Inputs relating to product requirements shall be determined and records maintained (see 4.2.4). These inputs shall include

a) functional and performance requirements,

b) applicable statutory and regulatory requirements,

c) where applicable, information derived from previous similar designs, and

d) other requirements essential for design and development.

These inputs shall be reviewed for adequacy. Requirements shall be complete, unambiguous and not in conflict with each other.

Source: ANSI/ISO/ASQ Q9001-2000

One of the often quoted, if ludicrous, criticisms of ISO 9001 is that it can be used to assure that a process is in place to produce conforming concrete life preservers. Whoever proffered this criticism did not understand the meaning of clause 7.3.2 (or its equivalent in ISO 9001:1994). This clause is intended to assure the development and documentation of a requirements specification or an equivalent statement of the general and specific characteristics of a product to be developed, including the suitability of the product to meet marketplace and customer needs.

There are many areas to consider when defining product requirements. Examples include statutory and regulatory requirements; environmental considerations such as ISO 14000; industry standards; national and international standards; organizational standards; safety regulations; customer wants and needs; cost; past experiences; and, for designs that are related to specific customer orders, contract commitments.

The result of the consideration of such items is the documentation of a complete and unambiguous statement of product requirements, sometimes called a requirements specification. Development work should not begin until such a document exists in a form acceptable to all who have responsibility for contributing to the product specification (at least to those who must bring the product to the marketplace as well as to those who must do the design and development). Concurrence with the requirements document by all parties is not required explicitly by clause 7.3.1, but it should be considered to avoid misunderstandings during project implementation. It is especially worthwhile to obtain closure, where appropriate, between marketing or sales and those who will be doing the development work. A requirements specification signed by the involved parties is one way to assure that concerned parties in an organization are in agreement regarding the product requirements. Such a document can provide the objective evidence of compliance with the requirements of this clause.

 ## DEFINITIONS

Product (3.4.2)—result of a **process** (3.4.1)

NOTE 1   There are four generic product categories, as follows:
—services (e.g. transport);
—software (e.g. computer program, dictionary);
—hardware (e.g. engine mechanical part);
—processed materials (e.g. lubricant).

Many products comprise elements belonging to different generic product categories. Whether the product is then called service, software, hardware or processed material depends on the dominant element. For example the offered product "automobile" consists of hardware (e.g. tyres), processed materials (e.g. fuel, cooling liquid), software (e.g. engine control software, driver's manual), and service (e.g. operating explanations given by the salesman).

NOTE 2   Service is the result of at least one activity necessarily performed at the interface between the **supplier** (3.3.6) and **customer** (3.3.5) and is generally intangible. Provision of a service can involve, for example, the following:

—an activity performed on a customer-supplied tangible product (e.g. automobile to be repaired);
—an activity performed on a customer-supplied intangible product (e.g. the income statement needed to prepare a tax return);
—the delivery of an intangible product (e.g. the delivery of information in the context of knowledge transmission);
—the creation of ambience for the customer (e.g. in hotels and restaurants).

Software consists of information and is generally intangible and can be in the form of approaches, transactions or **procedures** (3.4.5).

Hardware is generally tangible and its amount is a countable **characteristic** (3.5.1). Processed materials are generally tangible and their amount is a continuous characteristic. Hardware and processed materials often are referred to as goods.

NOTE 3   **Quality assurance** (3.2.11) is mainly focused on intended product.

Requirement (3.1.2)—need or expectation that is stated, generally implied or obligatory

NOTE 1   "Generally implied" means that it is custom or common practice for the **organization** (3.3.1), its **customers** (3.3.5) and other **interested parties** (3.3.7), that the need or expectation under consideration is implied.

NOTE 2   A qualifier can be used to denote a specific type of requirement, e.g. product requirement, quality management requirement, customer requirement.

NOTE 3   A specified requirement is one which is stated, for example, in a **document** (3.7.2).

NOTE 4   Requirements can be generated by different interested parties.

Source: ANSI/ISO/ASQ Q9000-2000

CONSIDERATIONS FOR DOCUMENTATION

Design and development inputs must be recorded. Later the design and development outputs must be provided in a form that permits verification against these inputs. This means careful thought should be given to the methods for determining and providing design and development inputs. Considerations should include:

- Creating a documented procedure that defines what will be recorded to ensure that product requirements are adequately defined and who will participate in the definition of product requirements

- Creating a procedure that defines the process for the review of product requirements for completeness and adequacy

This clause requires specific records of the design and development inputs. The planning for realization processes covered in clause 7.1 should include defining the records that the organization will keep during the process of developing the design and development inputs.

TYPICAL AUDIT ITEMS FOR COMPLIANCE

- Are requirements for new products defined and records maintained?
- Are the requirements complete?
- Are the requirements unambiguous?
- Are the requirements without conflict?

7.3.3 Design and development outputs

The outputs of design and development shall be provided in a form that enables verification against the design and development input and shall be approved prior to release.

Design and development outputs shall

a) meet the input requirements for design and development,

b) provide appropriate information for purchasing, production and for service provision,

c) contain or reference product acceptance criteria, and

d) specify the characteristics of the product that are essential for its safe and proper use.

Source: ANSI/ISO/ASQ Q9001-2000

This provision of the standard requires that design and development output be provided in a way that can be used for subsequent verification. This generally means there must be objective evidence that the design and development has been executed in accordance with the requirements that were defined at the inception of the project. The objective evidence can be in the form of development reports that contain data to show that the requirements have been satisfied, test results, or any other formal documentation of the results of the effort to develop a product with the specified characteristics. In some cases the output may include mock-ups, models, or other means to communicate the intent of the design and development team.

The conventional documentation of the results of a design and development project demonstrate that the product will do what it is expected to do. A more difficult issue to address with regard to design and development output is how to document that the product *will not do what it should not do.* It is especially important, for example, to assure that a software product will not interfere with the operation of other software.

The documentation of the results of a development project is typically the responsibility of the team or person who performed the work on the project.

In addition to documenting that the output results meet the input requirements, the standard requires that information be provided to facilitate product production. For hardware products this means that the design and development team or individual should provide appropriate information to facilitate the production of the product to specified requirements. For software products it is generally not necessary or pertinent to address item 7.3.3b—"provide appropriate information for purchasing, production and for service provision." For service products, however, it may be necessary to provide guidance to those in the organization who are responsible for producing collateral material that will be used in the delivery of the service (for example, training manuals).

Item 7.3.3c requires a clear and unambiguous statement of the requirements that a product must meet in order to be acceptable to customers. Such requirements will typically be incorporated into the test or inspection of the product to assure that the product will conform to defined customer needs. Providing clear product acceptance criteria from product design and development is essential for hardware, service, processed materials, and software products.

The output from the design and development process must "specify the characteristics of the product that are essential to its safe and proper use." The output from the design and development process is expected to include any information that relates to producing or using the product safely and properly. Organizations should pay particular attention to this issue. It not only addresses ultimate customer satisfaction with the product or service, but it also provides objective evidence that the organization considered the safe and proper use of products. The availability of such information could be important to demonstrating prudent judgment if there are liability issues related to the product or service. Conversely, not having such records could be viewed as evidence of a flawed design and development process.

Finally, the standard requires that the output from a design and development project be approved before the product is released. This requirement is included to assure that all aspects of the project have been executed in accordance with documented plans and applicable procedures before the product is launched into production or delivered to a customer.

 ## DEFINITIONS

Objective evidence (3.8.1)—data supporting the existence or verity of something

NOTE   Objective evidence may be obtained through observation, measurement, **test** (3.8.3), or other means.

Source: ANSI/ISO/ASQ Q9000-2000

 ## CONSIDERATIONS FOR DOCUMENTATION

The design and development outputs are normally documented, but whatever form the output takes, it must be in a form that can be used for subsequent design and development verification. Considerations should include defining in a documented procedure the expectations of developers about the form and content of the design and development output.

This clause does not require any specific records. But records in some form should exist to demonstrate compliance and to provide evidence of the use of prudent judgment in the design and development process.

TYPICAL AUDIT ITEMS FOR COMPLIANCE

- Is the output of design and development projects in a form suitable for verification against inputs?
- Does the design and development output satisfy input requirements (for example, as stated in a functional requirements specification)?
- Does output provide, as appropriate, information for purchasing, production operations, and service provision? Δ
- Are product acceptance criteria clearly stated?
- Are product safety and use characteristics identified?
- Is there an approval process for the release of products from the design and development process?

7.3.4 Design and development review

At suitable stages, systematic reviews of design and development shall be performed in accordance with planned arrangements (see 7.3.1)

a) to evaluate the ability of the results of design and development to meet requirements, and

b) to identify any problems and propose necessary actions.

Participants in such reviews shall include representatives of functions concerned with the design and development stage(s) being reviewed. Records of the results of the reviews and any necessary actions shall be maintained (see 4.2.4).

Source: ANSI/ISO/ASQ Q9001-2000

Design and development review is used to assure the timely release of a new product that fully meets the needs of the customers. It can also contribute significantly to reduced cost. The intent of the standard is to involve all appropriate individuals in the development of a new product as early as is feasible so that they can understand and address life-cycle issues early in the design and development process. Design and development review is intended to address more than just the question of whether the product will meet specified requirements. Design and development review is intended to address the "abilities" associated with a new product—manufacturability, deliverability, testability, inspectability, shipability, serviceability, repairability, availability, and reliability, as well as issues related to inventory and production planning and the purchase of components and subassemblies. Design and development reviews are intended to identify issues, to discuss possible resolutions, and to determine appropriate follow-up.

Design and development review is equally applicable to hardware, processed materials, software, and service projects. In fact, it is a critical element of the software design and development process. When robust design and development reviews are held for software projects, including design and development reviews of software test plans, development cycles are typically reduced and life-cycle costs are lower.

An important design and development review issue is to assure the design community that design review will not interfere with the creativity and innovation of the designers or slow down the development process. Rather, it is a process step intended to provide confidence that the spectrum of internal and external customer needs has been considered as early as possible and addressed with the aim of ultimately assuring external customer satisfaction.

The standard does not prescribe the number of design and development reviews that should be conducted. This should be determined during the design and development planning process and should be modified, as appropriate, during the course of a project. Certainly one design and development review is a minimum unless conditions warrant formally waiving this requirement. It may in certain circumstances be appropriate to waive this requirement, in which case there should be documentation of the reasons and the authority for the waiver, which should be included in the project files.

Records of design and development reviews must be maintained. The form of the documentation should suit the circumstances, but at a minimum it should include records of issues and proposed actions.

DEFINITIONS

Review (3.8.7)—activity undertaken to determine the suitability, adequacy and **effectiveness** (3.2.14) of the subject matter to achieve established objectives

NOTE Review can also include the determination of **efficiency** (3.2.15). EXAMPLE Management review, design and development review, review of customer requirements and nonconformity review.

Effectiveness (3.2.14)—extent to which planned activities are realized and planned results achieved

Efficiency (3.2.15)—relationship between the result achieved and the resources used

Source: ANSI/ISO/ASQ Q9000-2000

CONSIDERATIONS FOR DOCUMENTATION

Considerations should include defining a documented procedure for conducting design and development reviews, including who calls the reviews, who will attend, requirements for documenting the reviews, and requirements for follow-up on issues raised during reviews.

This clause requires records to be kept of design and development reviews. The clause has specific reference to clause 4.2.4 for control of the records generated. These records must include the results of the reviews and follow-up actions. Organizations should also consider including a description of what was included in each review and who conducted the review.

TYPICAL AUDIT ITEMS FOR COMPLIANCE

- Are design and development reviews being performed?
- Are they indicated in the project planning documents?
- Who attends?
- Is the attendance appropriate?
- Are results documented?
- Are follow-up actions taken?
- Are appropriate records maintained?

7.3.5 Design and development verification

Verification shall be performed in accordance with planned arrangements (see 7.3.1) to ensure that the design and development outputs have met the design and development input requirements. Records of the results of the verification and any necessary actions shall be maintained (see 4.2.4).

Source: ANSI/ISO/ASQ Q9001-2000

While this requirement is only two sentences long, it generates much misunderstanding. Verification is a distinct activity; it is different than validation. Both verification and validation were explicitly included in ISO 9001 in 1994, primarily to address the design element of the software sector, and both of these requirements have been retained in ISO 9001:2000.

Verification is a process step that can occur at various stages of the design and development process. It considers the product after the developers have completed work to assure that the output meets specified requirements. Verification makes a determination, by any reasonable means, that the product does meet the stated requirements. Verification can be done by review and analysis of test data, by making alternative calculations, by additional testing of the product or its components, or by any other means that the organization chooses.

If issues arise during verification activities, they must be documented, and follow-up actions need to be identified. Such actions may require rechecking of the output results against the input specifications and requirements and revalidating the product before release.

An important point is that the capability of the product to meet specified requirements is verified and that objective evidence exists to demonstrate the basis for this assertion. This requirement applies equally to all product sectors. The service sector should be particularly attentive to conducting thoughtful product verification, since the opportunity to address "nonconformity of product" after it is delivered to a customer usually does not exist. Service, even more than hardware or software, must be right the first time to maximize the probability of customer satisfaction.

 # DEFINITIONS

Verification (3.8.4)—confirmation, through the provision of **objective evidence** (3.8.1), that specified **requirements** (3.1.2) have been fulfilled

NOTE 1   The term "verified" is used to designate the corresponding status.
NOTE 2   Confirmation can comprise activities such as
—performing alternative calculations,
—comparing a new design **specification** (3.7.3) with a similar proven design specification,
—undertaking **tests** (3.8.3) and demonstrations, and
—reviewing documents prior to issue.

Source: ANSI/ISO/ASQ Q9000-2000

 # CONSIDERATIONS FOR DOCUMENTATION

A documented procedure should be considered for defining the verification process, including the following:

• Who does verification?
• How should results be recorded?

- How should follow-up of verification issues and reverification be managed?

This clause requires records of design and development verification results and subsequent follow-up actions. There is also specific reference to clause 4.2.4 for control of the records generated.

 TYPICAL AUDIT ITEMS FOR COMPLIANCE

- Is a verification process in place?
- Is it effectively implemented?
- Are follow-up actions recorded?
- Are required records defined and maintained?

7.3.6 Design and development validation

Design and development validation shall be performed in accordance with planned arrangements (see 7.3.1) to ensure that the resulting product is capable of meeting the requirements for the specified application or intended use, where known. Wherever practicable, validation shall be completed prior to the delivery or implementation of the product. Records of the results of validation and any necessary actions shall be maintained (see 4.2.4).

Source: ANSI/ISO/ASQ Q9001-2000

The difference between validation and verification of design and development output has caused much confusion in the past, especially with new users of the standard. As was indicated previously for the verification clause, both verification and validation were explicitly included in ISO 9001 in 1994 primarily to address the design element of the software sector, and both of these requirements have been retained in ISO 9001:2000.

Design and development validation is intended to assure that the design and development output conforms to defined user needs and "is capable of meeting the requirements for the specified application or intended use, where known." Design and development validation is usually performed after successful design and development verification. It is worthwhile to state again the difference between verification and validation. In simple language, *verification addresses conformance to requirements, while validation addresses meeting defined user needs.*

For hardware, if a water heater design meets all specified requirements but is not able to be easily installed by a plumber, it would "meet" the intent and requirement of the verification clause but not of the validation clause.

For software, if the output from a project to design a unit or module of a software product (for example, an SPC package) performed as specified in the SPC requirements specification but caused a word processor to crash when the SPC product was loaded into a system, then this product would "meet" the intent and requirement of the verification clause but not of the validation clause.

For service, the primary requirements might be met but secondary factors can suddenly overshadow them. Validation helps to uncover incomplete service requirements. For example, an express mail service that guarantees overnight delivery might meet the schedule, but it is inadequate if the package is left in a doorway during inclement weather and is destroyed by rain. This service would meet the intent and requirement of the verification clause but not of the validation clause.

It is especially important to understand and address validation in the world of software product development because of the often mysterious interactions that occur deep in the workings of a computer. In addition to being an ISO 9001 requirement, and even though software designers complain that there is never enough time to perform robust validation, this is not an area to be ignored or given perfunctory treatment.

In addition to the customer-satisfaction implications, robust validation processes are critical to optimizing the life-cycle costs of software (the majority of which typically occur after product release) and to minimizing product-liability exposure. Thus, validation should receive careful attention, and the results should be recorded and retained as records.

From the previous discussion, it is obvious that validation is performed after verification and in an environment that approximates as closely as possible the operating conditions that will exist in actual use. Also, whenever possible it should be performed before product is released for shipment. If it is not possible to perform a complete validation of a hardware, software, or service product before release and/or shipment to customers, then validation should be performed to the extent that is reasonable and final validation performed when and as appropriate.

In addition to customer-satisfaction issues, cost containment is a major reason for performing validation before a product is delivered to a customer. The resolution of issues after shipment can be very expensive.

 ## DEFINITIONS

Validation (3.8.5)—confirmation, through the provision of **objective evidence** (3.8.1), that the **requirements** (3.1.2) for a specific intended use or application have been fulfilled

NOTE 1   The term "validated" is used to designate the corresponding status.

NOTE 2   The use conditions for validation can be real or simulated.

Source: ANSI/ISO/ASQ Q9000-2000

 ## CONSIDERATIONS FOR DOCUMENTATION

Considerations should include documenting a process for performing design and development validation. Clause 7.3.6 requires records to be kept of the validation results and subsequent follow-up actions with specific reference to clause 4.2.4 on control of the records generated.

TYPICAL AUDIT ITEMS FOR COMPLIANCE

- Is design and development validation performed to confirm that the product is capable of meeting the requirements for intended use?
- Is validation completed prior to delivery when applicable?
- Are suitable controls provided in cases where full validation cannot be performed prior to delivery?
- Are records of design and development validation maintained?

7.3.7 Control of design and development changes

Design and development changes shall be identified and records maintained. The changes shall be reviewed, verified and validated, as appropriate, and approved before implementation. The review of design and development changes shall include evaluation of the effect of the changes on constituent parts and product already delivered.

Records of the results of the review of changes and any necessary actions shall be maintained (see 4.2.4).

Source: ANSI/ISO/ASQ Q9001-2000

During the course of a design and development project, there are usually changes to the requirements that were defined at the input stage. Such changes occur for many reasons, including: (1) omissions that become apparent after design and development work starts, (2) errors or inconsistencies in the design or in a specification requirement, (3) changes requested by marketing or by a customer, (4) perceived improvement opportunities, (5) changing regulatory or statutory conditions, (6) issues raised in design and development review, (7) issues raised during the verification process, and (8) issues raised during the validation process.

Any changes that occur in the design of a product, either during the design and development process, during production, or after the delivery of the product to a customer, "shall be identified and records maintained." This requirement applies to all product sectors and especially to software, where configuration control is a major issue.

Changes to a product should be viewed as miniprojects within a project. The reason for this is that any changes, even those perceived as "improvements," can have unforeseen adverse effects on other elements of a product or can result in unanticipated system performance when used in a real-life environment. Therefore, changes should be exercised through design and development review, verification, and validation processes.

This clause also now requires evaluation of the effect of changes and follow-up actions, if necessary.

 ## CONSIDERATIONS FOR DOCUMENTATION

Consideration should be given to documenting procedures to assure that design and development project changes are communicated to all interested parties, that all changes are recorded, that document processing and control are adequate (see chapter 2), and that appropriate authorization is documented for any changes.

This clause requires documentation of the results of the review of changes and subsequent follow-up. The clause also has a specific reference to clause 4.2.4 for control of the records generated. Design and development changes must be reflected in the design and development output documents. Records must also be kept of the design-change reviews themselves and follow-up actions taken.

 ## TYPICAL AUDIT ITEMS FOR COMPLIANCE

Items representing a difference from ISO 9001:1994 have a Δ at the end.

- Are all design and development project changes documented and reviewed?
- Are design and development changes verified and validated, as appropriate? Δ
- Is there evidence to demonstrate that changes are authorized?
- Do records include the results of reviews of changes?
- Have changes been communicated to interested parties?
- Do records include follow-up actions related to the review of changes? Δ

CHAPTER

7

Purchasing

7.4 Purchasing

7.4.1 Purchasing process

The organization shall ensure that purchased product conforms to specified purchase requirements. The type and extent of control applied to the supplier and the purchased product shall be dependent upon the effect of the purchased product on subsequent product realization or the final product.

The organization shall evaluate and select suppliers based on their ability to supply product in accordance with the organization's requirements. Criteria for selection, evaluation and re-evaluation shall be established. Records of the results of evaluations and any necessary actions arising from the evaluation shall be maintained (see 4.2.4).

Source: ANSI/ISO/ASQ Q9001-2000

The requirements described in clause 7.4 are similar in intent and content to the requirements contained in clause 4.6 in ISO 9001:1994.

The 2000 standard permits the organization to decide the "type and extent of control," which should be based on the effect of the purchased material on the product realization processes and on the products produced. If purchased material has little impact, then minimal control is needed (for example, a bolt that is used inside a noncritical subassembly). Generally speaking, minimal control is required for commodity-type purchased material.

If purchased material has high actual or high potential impact on either the final product or the realization processes, then more robust control is required. If, for example, the bolt mentioned previously is used for an aircraft engine mount, then the controls will be more extensive than if the bolt is used in a noncritical application inside a subassembly.

Determining the nature of the control is the responsibility of the organization as it considers customer, regulatory, industry, and other appropriate requirements. ISO 9001:2000 requires the organization to think about what makes sense from both a customer and a business perspective.

The standard still requires the organization to evaluate suppliers and to define the criteria used to select and periodically evaluate suppliers. It also adds a requirement for establishing criteria for the reevaluation of suppliers. However, the organization has broad flexibility regarding how to do this and can focus more on obtaining conforming material rather than on maintaining approved-supplier lists. As before, the results of all evaluations and any required follow-up actions shall be documented and retained as records.

 ## DEFINITIONS

Requirement (3.1.2)—need or expectation that is stated, generally implied or obligatory

NOTE 1   "Generally implied" means that it is custom or common practice for the **organization** (3.3.1), its **customers** (3.3.5) and other **interested parties** (3.3.7), that the need or expectation under consideration is implied.

NOTE 2   A qualifier can be used to denote a specific type of requirement, e.g. product requirement, quality management requirement, customer requirement.

NOTE 3   A specified requirement is one which is stated, for example, in a **document** (3.7.2).

NOTE 4   Requirements can be generated by different interested parties.

Supplier (3.3.6)—**organization** (3.3.1) or person that provides a **product** (3.4.2)

EXAMPLE   Producer, distributor, retailer or vendor of a product, or provider of a service or information.

NOTE 1   A supplier can be internal or external to the organization.

NOTE 2   In a contractual situation a supplier is sometimes called "contractor".

Source: ANSI/ISO/ASQ Q9000-2000

 ## CONSIDERATIONS FOR DOCUMENTATION

Organizations should consider documented procedures to describe processes for the selection and periodic evaluation of suppliers. Organizations should also carefully consider how they will communicate their processes for controlling

purchased material that will affect customer satisfaction. Typically, they will document the process to be used in the form of a written procedure to assure that the requirements are understood and consistently implemented.

Clause 7.4.1 requires records of the results of supplier evaluations and subsequent follow-up actions, with specific reference to clause 4.2.4 for control of the records generated. These records would include reports of supplier evaluations, corrective actions requested of suppliers, and the actual corrective actions taken.

 ## TYPICAL AUDIT ITEMS FOR COMPLIANCE

Items representing a difference from ISO 9001:1994 have a Δ at the end.

- Have criteria for the selection and periodic evaluation of suppliers been defined? Δ
- Is there a process for selecting and evaluating suppliers?
- Are the results of evaluations documented and retained as records?

7.4.2 Purchasing information

Purchasing information shall describe the product to be purchased, including where appropriate

a) requirements for approval of product, procedures, processes and equipment,

b) requirements for qualification of personnel, and

c) quality management system requirements.

The organization shall ensure the adequacy of specified purchase requirements prior to their communication to the supplier.

Source: ANSI/ISO/ASQ Q9001-2000

The intent of this requirement is essentially unchanged from 1994. The language used is more general, however, so that it can be applied to all product sectors. It states that purchasing documents (for example, purchase orders) should provide the information needed to clearly communicate to suppliers what the organization wants to purchase. The requirement indicates the various types of information that may be pertinent and indicates that these items shall be considered as appropriate.

This clause also requires a process to assure that purchasing documents adequately state all of the requirements for the items to be purchased. This can be accomplished by a process as simple as a sign-off of a purchase order or by a more elaborate process that can involve several layers of review and approval, especially for high-value purchased items. Organizations that execute web-based purchasing transactions will need to devise creative approaches to address the requirement for assuring the adequacy of purchase requirements. Perhaps a simple checkbox on the electronic transmission of an "order" indicating that the order has been reviewed before transmission would suffice.

 ## DEFINITIONS

Release (3.6.13)—permission to proceed to the next stage of a **process** (3.4.1)

NOTE   In English, in the context of computer software, the term "release" is frequently used to refer to a version of the software itself.

Source: ANSI/ISO/ASQ Q9000-2000.

 ## CONSIDERATIONS FOR DOCUMENTATION

Considerations for documentation should include the development of a documented procedure that defines what to include in purchasing documents. Organizations should also consider the need for a written procedure that defines an approval process for review and approval of purchasing documents before release to suppliers. Clause 7.4.2 also does not require any specific records. The planning for realization processes covered in clause 7.1 should define the records the organization will keep. Consider keeping records of the purchased-material document review and copies of the purchase documents themselves.

 TYPICAL AUDIT ITEMS FOR COMPLIANCE

- Do purchasing documents adequately describe the products being ordered?
- Do purchasing documents include, where appropriate, requirements for approval or qualification of product, procedures, processes, equipment, and personnel?
- Do purchasing documents include, where applicable, quality management system requirements?
- How does the organization assure the adequacy of specified purchase requirements prior to communication to the supplier?

7.4.3 Verification of purchased product

The organization shall establish and implement the inspection or other activities necessary for ensuring that purchased product meets specified purchase requirements.

Where the organization or its customer intends to perform verification at the supplier's premises, the organization shall state the intended verification arrangements and method of product release in the purchasing information.

Source: ANSI/ISO/ASQ Q9001-2000

There are two distinct requirements in clause 7.4.3. The first is a requirement to assure that purchased material conforms to requirements. In ISO 9001:1994, receiving inspection and test of purchased material was addressed in clause 4.10.2. In the 2000 standard, the requirements are considerably streamlined, and the organization has much more discretion and flexibility in assuring that purchased product conforms to requirements. Nevertheless, a process is required that can include approaches such as the following:

- Certifying suppliers (based on demonstrated performance or process capability) and requiring no inspection or test
- Conventional incoming inspection using sampling plans
- One hundred percent inspection (or more)
- Verification at the supplier's facility
- Any combination of these or other approaches

Whatever methods are used, the verification activities must be planned and effectively implemented.

Verification of purchased product is directed at purchased product that will be incorporated into the products the organization delivers to customers, not the entire spectrum of products purchased by the organization (for example, pencils, rock salt, and so on would be outside the scope of this clause).

Performing verification activities at the supplier's premises is not common for many organizations. If this is the case, a simple statement in the quality management system documentation specifying that "this requirement does not apply and if such a situation ever arises, the organization shall prepare a unique quality plan to address the situation" will suffice to meet this requirement. If performing verification activities at the supplier's premises is an applicable requirement, then the purchasing documents should describe the procedures to be followed along with the criteria for the release of product by the supplier.

 DEFINITIONS

Verification (3.8.4)—confirmation, through the provision of **objective evidence** (3.8.1), that specified **requirements** (3.1.2) have been fulfilled

NOTE 1   The term "verified" is used to designate the corresponding status.

NOTE 2   Confirmation can comprise activities such as
—performing alternative calculations,
—comparing a new design **specification** (3.7.3) with a similar proven design specification,
—undertaking **tests** (3.8.3) and demonstrations, and
—reviewing documents prior to issue.

Source: ANSI/ISO/ASQ Q9000-2000

CONSIDERATIONS FOR DOCUMENTATION

Considerations should include the process for identifying and implementing the activities necessary to assure conformance of purchased product. If verification activities are performed at the supplier's premises, consider preparing a documented procedure for performing this verification and for release of the product. This clause also does not require any specific records. The planning for realization processes covered in clause 7.1 should define the records the organization will keep. Consideration should be given to keeping records of product verification and product release.

TYPICAL AUDIT ITEMS FOR COMPLIANCE

- Has the organization defined a process for verifying that purchased product conforms to defined requirements?
- Is the process effectively implemented?
- Does objective evidence exist of product acceptance?
- Is verification of purchased product performed at the supplier's premises? If so, are the arrangements specified and does objective evidence exist of effective implementation?

CHAPTER

8

Production and Service Provision

7.5 Production and service provision

7.5.1 Control of production and service provision

The organization shall plan and carry out production and service provision under controlled conditions. Controlled conditions shall include, as applicable

a) the availability of information that describes the characteristics of the product,

b) the availability of work instructions, as necessary,

c) the use of suitable equipment,

d) the availability and use of monitoring and measuring devices,

e) the implementation of monitoring and measurement, and

f) the implementation of release, delivery and post-delivery activities.

Source: ANSI/ISO/ASQ Q9001-2000

The total set of requirements pertaining to *production and service provision* is not much different from the requirements of the 1994 standard. The term *provision* is used in its common dictionary sense: the act of providing. This clause encompasses production and service operations. It appears to contain fewer requirements than the corresponding clauses of the previous standard because all of the requirements for production and service provision are not listed in clause 7.5. Instead, common requirements are now stated only once and are not repeated throughout the standard in order to eliminate redundancy and to simplify the presentation of requirements. This is particularly evident in clause 7.5.1, *Control of production and service provision,* which encompasses the requirements from four clauses of ISO 9001:1994 (clauses 4.9, 4.10, 4.12, and 4.19).

Documentation requirements for the overall quality management system are stated in clause 4 and are not repeated here. Likewise, clause 7.1 addresses the planning of product realization processes and requires that they be documented in a manner suitable for the organization's method of operation. Process and product-measurement requirements are stated in clause 8.2.3 and clause 8.2.4. ISO 9001:2000 emphasizes the process approach for the entire quality management system. There is a clear need to view the entire interconnected quality management system, not a collection of individual, standalone elements.

The requirements are expressed in more general terms that provide greater clarity as to their meaning for software and service providers. Although these appear in a more general format, they should not be interpreted as lessened or weakened requirements for hardware producers or providers of processed materials.

The focus of clause 7.5.1, *Control of production and service provision,* is on the key concept that processes need to be carried out under controlled conditions. The exact words in ISO 9001:2000 parallel those in Clause 4.9 of ISO 9001:1994: "The organization shall plan and carry out production and service provision under controlled conditions." Considerations for achieving controlled conditions are presented. The requirements to determine the extent to which production and service operations are planned, established, documented, verified, and validated are presented in clause 7.1. Since clause 7.1 applies to all of the realization processes, these planning and development requirements are not repeated.

The organization should control process operations by considering a number of factors. This begins with understanding the specifications of the product that the processes need to produce or realize. The organization must determine the production and service processes that need to be controlled and the outputs that must be achieved at each stage of processing.

Also, the specific items of equipment that are needed to achieve the product specifications, including their sequence and operating conditions, need to be addressed.

The organization needs to determine the criteria of acceptability for these processes and needs to perform evaluations against these criteria (see clause 7.1). One approach is to perform capability studies to demonstrate process suitability. From the determination of suitability, decisions can be made if additional process development effort is required to achieve the product specifications. Appropriate criteria and controls for these processes need to be determined and implemented to maintain process capability and to prevent nonconformities from occurring. The corresponding work instructions and the associated measurement equipment should be identified. In determining the extent of documentation needed, the organization should consider the criticality of the product, the competency of its people, and the complexity and size of the organization. Controls often include direct measurement of process parameters and characteristics. There may be inspection or test of the output of the process (for example, the product or service). In some cases, both may be used. Whichever combination of approaches is adopted, verification activities should be integrated to maximize both the efficiency of the verification and confidence in the product. Overall, this clause requires organizations to think about their operations.

SERVICES

Every service organization should be aware of the requirements and conditions for the proper operation of its planned and offered services and should establish these in writing. One approach is to rank the offered services in the order of their importance, cost, and criticality. The task of the organization is to plan, monitor, and systematically supervise the fulfillment of services so that the quality objectives can be achieved. For some types of services, there is little or no process equipment to control, as the service consists of actions performed by the service personnel directly for or with the customer. In these cases, the requirements of this clause apply directly to the service personnel and to the processes that control their competence (see chapter 4).

As appropriate, release methods need to be developed and implemented before providing the service to the customer. The release methods differ in form, timing, and application. For example, airline pilots use preflight checklists to verify that requirements have been met prior to takeoff. An automobile repair shop uses both test instruments and a test drive to verify the satisfactory completion of its service before releasing a repaired vehicle to the customer. Also, customer-contact employees can receive immediate feedback by asking customers if the services have been adequately provided.

HARDWARE AND PROCESSED MATERIALS

Raw materials, parts, and subassemblies should conform to appropriate specifications before being introduced into processing. In determining the amount of testing or inspection necessary, organizations should compare the cost of evaluation at various stages to the added value of subsequent activities. The economic impact of discarding or reworking product should be considered when planning the controls. In-process materials should be appropriately stored, segregated, handled, and protected to maintain their suitability. Special consideration should be given to shelf life and the potential for deterioration. Where in-plant traceability of material is important to quality, appropriate identification should be maintained throughout processing to ensure traceability to original material identification and quality status. Where important to quality characteristics, auxiliary materials and utilities such as water, compressed air, electric power, and chemicals used for processing should be controlled and verified periodically to ensure uniformity of effect on the process. Where a work environment (such as temperature, humidity, and cleanliness) is important to product and service quality, appropriate limits should be specified, controlled, and verified (see chapter 4).

SOFTWARE

The creation of software code is usually part of the design and development process. Mass production of software simply involves replicating the code. Nevertheless, it is essential to control the final stages of development through to code replication and subsequent installation and servicing processes.

In this area, configuration management is very important. The process controls should include documented procedures for configuration management to the extent appropriate. This discipline should have been initiated early in the design phase and should continue through the life cycle of the software. It assists in the control of design, development, provision, and use of the software, and it enables the organization to examine the state of the software during its life. Configuration management can include configuration identification, configuration control, configuration status accounting, and configuration audit.

 DEFINITIONS

Capability (3.1.5)—ability of an **organization** (3.3.1), **system** (3.2.1) or **process** (3.4.1) to realize a **product** (3.4.2) that will fulfil the **requirements** (3.1.2) for that product

NOTE   Process capability terms in the field of statistics are defined in ISO 3534-2.

Characteristic (3.5.1)—distinguishing feature

NOTE 1   A characteristic can be inherent or assigned.

NOTE 2   A characteristic can be qualitative or quantitative.

NOTE 3   There are various classes of characteristic, such as the following:

—physical (e.g. mechanical, electrical, chemical or biological characteristics);

—sensory (e.g. related to smell, touch, taste, sight, hearing);

—behavioral (e.g. courtesy, honesty, veracity);

—temporal (e.g. punctuality, reliability, availability);

—ergonomic (e.g. physiological characteristic, or related to human safety);

—functional (e.g. maximum speed of an aircraft).

Process (3.4.1)—set of interrelated or interacting activities which transforms inputs into outputs

NOTE 1   Inputs to a process are generally outputs of other processes.

NOTE 2   Processes in an **organization** (3.3.1) are generally planned and carried out under controlled conditions to add value.

NOTE 3   A process where the **conformity** (3.6.1) of the resulting **product** (3.4.2) cannot be readily or economically verified is frequently referred to as a "special process".

Quality characteristic (3.5.2)—inherent **characteristic** (3.5.1) of a **product** (3.4.2), **process** (3.4.1) or **system** (3.2.1) related to a **requirement** (3.1.2)

NOTE 1   Inherent means existing in something, especially as a permanent characteristic.

NOTE 2   A characteristic assigned to a product, process or system (e.g. the price of a product, the owner of a product) is not a quality characteristic of that product, process or system.

Release (3.6.13)—permission to proceed to the next stage of a **process** (3.4.1)

NOTE   In English, in the context of computer software, the term "release" is frequently used to refer to a version of the software itself.

Requirement (3.1.2)—need or expectation that is stated, generally implied or obligatory

NOTE 1   "Generally implied" means that it is custom or common practice for the **organization** (3.3.1), its **customers** (3.3.5) and other **interested parties** (3.3.7), that the need or expectation under consideration is implied.

NOTE 2   A qualifier can be used to denote a specific type of requirement, e.g. product requirement, quality management requirement, customer requirement.

NOTE 3   A specified requirement is one which is stated, for example, in a **document** (3.7.2).

NOTE 4   Requirements can be generated by different interested parties.

Specification (3.7.3)—**document** (3.7.2) stating **requirements** (3.1.2)

NOTE   A specification can be related to activities (e.g. procedure document, process specification and test specification), or **products** (3.4.2) (e.g. product specification, performance specification and drawing).

Verification (3.8.4)—confirmation, through the provision of **objective evidence** (3.8.1), that specified **requirements** (3.1.2) have been fulfilled

NOTE 1   The term "verified" is used to designate the corresponding status.

NOTE 2   Confirmation can comprise activities such as
—performing alternative calculations,

—comparing a new design **specification** (3.7.3) with a similar proven design specification,

—undertaking **tests** (3.8.3) and demonstrations, and

—reviewing documents prior to issue.

Work environment (3.3.4)—set of conditions under which work is performed

NOTE   Conditions include physical, social, psychological and environmental factors (such as temperature, recognition schemes, ergonomics and atmospheric composition).

Source: ANSI/ISO/ASQ Q9000-2000

CONSIDERATIONS FOR DOCUMENTATION

There is a specific requirement for the implementation of a defined process for release, delivery, and applicable post-delivery activities. An easy way of defining such processes is through the use of documented procedures. Considerations should include the development and documentation of needed procedures and work instructions.

TYPICAL AUDIT ITEMS FOR COMPLIANCE

* Are specifications available that define quality characteristic requirements of the product or service?

* Has the organization determined the criteria of acceptability for demonstrating the suitability of equipment for production and service operations to meet product or service specifications?

* Has the organization demonstrated the suitability of equipment for production and service operations to meet product or service specifications?

* Has the organization defined all production and service provision activities that require control, including those that need ongoing monitoring, work instructions, or special controls?

* Are work instructions available and adequate to permit control of the appropriate operations so as to ensure conformity of the product or service?

- Have the requirements for the work environment needed to ensure the conformity of the product or service been defined and are these work environment requirements being met?

- Is suitable monitoring and measurement equipment available when and where necessary to ensure conformity of the product or service?

- Have monitoring and measurement activities been planned and are they carried out as required?

- For hardware, processed material, and software have suitable processes been implemented for release of the product and for its delivery to the customer?

- Have suitable release mechanisms been put in place to ensure that product and service conforms to requirements?

7.5.2 Validation of processes for production and service provision

The organization shall validate any processes for production and service provision where the resulting output cannot be verified by subsequent monitoring or measurement. This includes any processes where deficiencies become apparent only after the product is in use or the service has been delivered.

Validation shall demonstrate the ability of these processes to achieve planned results.

The organization shall establish arrangements for these processes including, as applicable

a) defined criteria for review and approval of the processes,

b) approval of equipment and qualification of personnel,

c) use of specific methods and procedures,

d) requirements for records (see 4.2.4), and

e) revalidation.

Source: ANSI/ISO/ASQ Q9001-2000

Although text changes have been made to provide added clarity, all of the requirements of the 1994 standard remain.

Ultimately, the output of processes should provide finished product that meets the customer requirements. Many finished products do not present any difficulty for verification against end-user requirements through visual inspection, direct measurement of product characteristics, or testing of performance. For processes used to create these products, the extent to which all of the production and service processes require validation is based on practical and economic factors. It is always in the best interest of the organization to develop and implement processes that are fully capable of meeting finished-product requirements; by so doing, the organization minimizes or eliminates the creation of nonconforming product that would need to be reprocessed or discarded. To demonstrate that this has been achieved, organizations often validate all major processes. There is a common expression that it is always less expensive to make the product right the first time. From a practical standpoint, the organization must find the best balance between product verification and process validation.

When the processes are such that the achievement of the product specifications cannot be fully verified by the examination of finished product, either at an earlier stage of production or after finishing, process validation must be performed. Inability to fully verify every unit of product may be due to the nature of the testing (for example, when the testing is destructive). In such cases, the process must be validated. Records of validation need to be established and maintained, as appropriate.

 There is now a requirement for defining the conditions and criteria for revalidation. After being validated, processes must be maintained in a validated state. If changes are made to the process equipment, the product design, the materials used to produce the product, or to other significant factors such as new personnel, the process often requires revalidation. The organization therefore needs to define the conditions that require a revalidation to be performed. Even if no initiating events occur, common practice often requires revalidation after a minimum period of use. In some industries, revalidation is required if a period of five years has elapsed without an intervening validation. Validation should be carried out at appropriate intervals to respond to changes in market requirements, regulations, or standards in addition to assuring the continued acceptable performance of processes.

SERVICES

Examples of service processes requiring validation include those processes that create financial or legal documents and those that deal with professional advice. Validation includes considering a number of factors such as the need to qualify the processing method, the qualifying of service equipment, and having qualified personnel providing the service.

HARDWARE AND PROCESSED MATERIALS

Examples of typical processes for hardware or processed materials that require validation include welding, soldering, gluing, casting, forging, heat treating, and forming processes. Products with quality characteristics that require certain test and inspection techniques for verification such as nondestructive examinations (e.g. radiographic, eddy current, or ultrasonic examination), environmental testing, or mechanical stress tests usually require process validation. Validation includes consideration of the qualification of equipment, personnel, and processes.

SOFTWARE

Generally, software—even the simplest of codes—cannot be fully verified through testing. The expectations are that all software needs to be created by controlled processes following the model described in clause 7.3. The methods and extent of the process validations will differ widely based on the criticality and use of the software. The qualification of personnel, equipment, and software development methodologies and procedures is an important aspect of assuring that software conforms to specified requirements.

DEFINITIONS

Verification (3.8.4)—confirmation, through the provision of **objective evidence** (3.8.1), that specified **requirements** (3.1.2) have been fulfilled

NOTE 1   The term "verified" is used to designate the corresponding status.
NOTE 2   Confirmation can comprise activities such as
—performing alternative calculations,
—comparing a new design **specification** (3.7.3) with a similar proven design specification,
—undertaking **tests** (3.8.3) and demonstrations, and
—reviewing documents prior to issue.

Validation (3.8.5)—confirmation, through the provision of **objective evidence** (3.8.1), that the **requirements** (3.1.2) for a specific intended use or application have been fulfilled

NOTE 1   The term "validated" is used to designate the corresponding status.
NOTE 2   The use conditions for validation can be real or simulated.

Source: ANSI/ISO/ASQ Q9000-2000

CONSIDERATIONS FOR DOCUMENTATION

Clause 7.5.2 requires that the organization define the arrangements for the validation of processes. Organizations should consider defining these arrangements in a written procedure. This clause requires applicable records. The planning for realization processes covered in clause 7.1 should define the records the organization will keep. Clause 7.5.2 requires the organization to define any records that are to be kept as a part of process validation. Organizations should consider keeping records of personnel and equipment qualifications where such qualifications are required.

TYPICAL AUDIT ITEMS FOR COMPLIANCE

Items representing a difference from ISO 9001:1994 have a Δ at the end.

- Has the organization determined which production or service processes require validation? Have these processes been validated?

- Has the organization defined criteria for the review and approval of production or service processes? Have the reviews and approvals been performed?

- Has the organization determined what personnel need to be qualified and has it determined the qualification criteria? Have these personnel been qualified?

- Does the organization use defined methods and procedures to validate processes?

- Have the requirements for records of validated processes been defined?

- Are records of validated processes maintained?

- Have the processes requiring revalidation been defined? Δ

- Have processes, as required, been revalidated? Δ

- Do adequate records exist to assure that process validation is effectively implemented?

7.5.3 Identification and traceability

Where appropriate, the organization shall identify the product by suitable means throughout product realization.

The organization shall identify the product status with respect to monitoring and measurement requirements.

Where traceability is a requirement, the organization shall control and record the unique identification of the product (see 4.2.4).

NOTE   In some industry sectors, configuration management is a means by which identification and traceability are maintained.

Source: ANSI/ISO/ASQ Q9001-2000

Requirements in this clause are equivalent to those in the 1994 standard. The identification requirements that were in the clause for inspection and test status (clause 4.12 in ISO 9001:1994), have now been combined with this product identification and traceability clause. The standard has been rearranged to present an integrated system and to minimize redundant text. As noted for this entire section, documentation requirements are now contained in clauses 4 and 7.1.

Identification and traceability are separate but related issues. The degree of product identification that is needed must be determined, including any requirements for tracking purchased components, materials, and supplies that are uniquely related to the product. Appropriateness depends upon the nature of the product, the nature and complexity of the process, industry practice, and whether identification is required in a contract. Integral to product identification is its status in meeting requirements at various stages of production or service development, storage, and delivery as indicated by passing tests and inspections.

In order to trace a product, the organization must identify the product and its component parts in adequate detail. Thus, traceability is closely related to identification. Full traceability involves the ability to trace the history, application, or location of an item or activity. This is usually required when there is a need to trace a problem back to its source and when it is necessary to be able to isolate all parts of an affected batch. Records that are needed to ensure traceability should be defined. For example, traceability is typically a contract requirement for certain medical devices, for defense/space vehicle assemblies, and for devices used in nuclear power plants.

SERVICES

It may be important to identify specific personnel involved in each phase of a service delivery process. Different personnel may be involved in successive service functions, each of which is to be traceable. For example, the recording through signatures on serially numbered documents in banking operations is often required. In this case, there is no tangible product, but each person's identity needs to be traceable to provide the appropriate documentation trail. In a different application, signatures often serve as indications of processing status and approval to proceed with payment of, for example, an invoice.

HARDWARE AND PROCESSED MATERIALS

Product identification is often achieved by marking or tagging a product or its container. When products are visually identical but their functional characteristics are different, different markings or colors may be used. More often, quantities of product are segregated into batches with unique batch numbers. Batch definition may be determined by identifying potential sources of batch-to-batch variation. Sources of variation traditionally are the five Ms of man (operator), method (or procedure), material, measurement (measurement method and instrument), and machine (or processing step). New batches may be defined as these potential sources change. Traceability approaches vary widely and depend on the application regarding how the unique identification of product is accomplished.

SOFTWARE

Software configuration management practices require that each version of a configuration item be identified by some appropriate means. Likewise, there is a need to maintain the status of the verification steps and tests that have been completed. The results achieved by the product or product components at each phase of the development cycle must also be maintained.

 ## DEFINITIONS

Traceability (3.5.4)—ability to trace the history, application or location of that which is under consideration

NOTE 1   When considering **product** (3.4.2), traceability can relate to
—the origin of materials and parts,
—the processing history, and
—the distribution and location of the product after delivery.

NOTE 2   In the field of metrology the definition in VIM:1993, 6.10, is the accepted definition.

Source: ANSI/ISO/ASQ Q9000-2000

CONSIDERATIONS FOR DOCUMENTATION

Documentation considerations should include a documented procedure for maintaining identification and for control of product status. Where there are specific requirements for unique identity, the organization should consider preparing a documented procedure to describe how this is accomplished and recorded. This clause requires records of unique identification in cases where traceability is required.

TYPICAL AUDIT ITEMS FOR COMPLIANCE

- Has the product been identified by suitable means throughout production and service operations?
- Has the status of the product been identified at suitable stages with respect to monitoring and measurement requirements?
- Is traceability a requirement?
- Where traceability is a requirement, is the unique identification of the product recorded and controlled?

7.5.4 Customer property

The organization shall exercise care with customer property while it is under the organization's control or being used by the organization. The organization shall identify, verify, protect and safeguard customer property provided for use or incorporation into the product. If any customer property is lost, damaged or otherwise found to be unsuitable for use, this shall be reported to the customer and records maintained (see 4.2.4).

NOTE   Customer property can include intellectual property.

Source: ANSI/ISOASQ Q9001-2000

Customer property is product that is owned by the customer and furnished to the organization for use in meeting the requirements of the agreement between the two. Upon receipt of the product from the customer, the organization agrees to safeguard the product while it is in the organization's possession.

There are no significant differences in requirements from the previous standard. There is clarification that the requirements for the control of customer property include all property provided by the customer, including such items as tooling, information, test software, and shipping containers.

One requirement from the 1994 standard that appears to have been dropped is that the customer must provide acceptable product. Of course this is still necessary, but such wording can be confusing. It was agreed that this requirement does not belong in the standard. It should be part of the agreement between the organization and the customer and, if needed, is better defined in contractual documents. It is fundamental that the customer will provide product that is acceptable for the purpose provided. However, if this is product that needs to be repaired, for example, it would need to be acceptable for repair. If not, the organization might return the product to the customer as not repairable. A contractual business relationship, written or understood, should deal with this situation.

The note makes it clear that information or other intellectual property is a type of customer property.

SERVICES

In many cases this requirement entails a service provided by the organization to the customer. Repair of a piece of equipment requires clearly defining the responsibilities of both parties. An automotive repair shop must not damage a customer's car. On a much larger scale, shipowners contract for the repair of ships with private shipbuilders using owner-furnished equipment and owner-furnished material for a ship that often is to arrive at some future date. Equipment and material may be held in inventory before and after repairs are completed by the private shipbuilder. The storage and handling of supplied material must be considered.

HARDWARE AND PROCESSED MATERIALS

Upon receipt of a product, the organization should examine it to check for identity, quantity, and damage. The product should be safeguarded and maintained. The organization may need to provide maintenance or utilize a maintenance contract with a third party. In such cases, the contractual agreements need to be clear as to responsibility.

SOFTWARE

This clause can be a significant factor in operations dealing with software. An example is the case where a customer provides source code to a contract programming organization for modification to incorporate additional features. The organization must exercise care in protecting the original functionality of the software. Detailed agreements typically define these relationships, including verification and validation requirements of the changes.

 DEFINITIONS

Verification (3.8.4)—confirmation, through the provision of **objective evidence** (3.8.1), that specified **requirements** (3.1.2) have been fulfilled

NOTE 1   The term "verified" is used to designate the corresponding status.
NOTE 2   Confirmation can comprise activities such as
—performing alternative calculations,
—comparing a new design **specification** (3.7.3) with a similar proven design specification,
—undertaking **tests** (3.8.3) and demonstrations, and
—reviewing documents prior to issue.

Source: ANSI/ISO/ASQ Q9000-2000

CONSIDERATIONS FOR DOCUMENTATION

Whether or not a documented procedure is needed depends upon the nature of customer property, the control requirements laid out by the customer (if any), and the nature and size of the organization. So, for example, it is not always necessary to have a documented procedure for the protection of confidential information provided verbally by a customer. Also, if the confidential information is provided in a few documents, it may not be necessary to have documented procedures if the organization is a small consulting firm with a single administrative assistant handling and storing all documents. If, on the other hand, the organization is a large corporation with many people potentially handling the documents, it may be appropriate to have documented procedures defining their control.

This clause requires records to be kept of customer property that is lost, damaged, or found to be unsuitable. The purpose for recording the loss, damage, or unsuitable condition is to report it to the customer. Organizations would be well advised to keep copies of these reports as controlled records.

TYPICAL AUDIT ITEMS FOR COMPLIANCE

- Has the organization identified, verified, protected, and maintained customer property that is provided for incorporation into the product?

- Does control extend to all customer property, including intellectual property?

- Does the organization have records that indicate when customer property has been lost, damaged, or otherwise found to be unsuitable?

- Is there evidence that when customer property has been lost, damaged, or otherwise found to be unsuitable that the customer has been informed? Are records maintained?

7.5.5 Preservation of product

The organization shall preserve the conformity of product during internal processing and delivery to the intended destination. This preservation shall include identification, handling, packaging, storage and protection. Preservation shall also apply to the constituent parts of a product.

Source: ANSI/ISO/ASQ Q9001-2000

This clause replaces the 1994 requirements for *Handling, storage, packaging, preservation and delivery.* These requirements have not been changed in intent, in scope, or in detail of implementation. For those organizations that have a quality system in place that meets these requirements from the 1994 standard, no changes are needed. The written requirements in the standard have been simplified to make them more appropriate for all types of organizations and all types of products. The 1994 requirements were written in language easily understood by organizations producing hardware and processed materials. There were significant comments from service providers about the inappropriateness of the 1994 text for their applications.

The organization must safeguard and protect the product during and between all processing steps through to delivery. It should have a system for appropriately identifying, handling, packaging, storing, and delivering the product, including its components.

Marking and labeling should be readable, visually or by machine. Consideration should be given to documented procedures for segregating batches, stock rotation, and expiration dates. Packaging, containers, wraps, and pallets should be appropriate and durable for protecting the product from damage. Suitable storage facilities that include both physical security and protection from the environment should be provided. It may be necessary to check product periodically to detect deterioration. The organization should provide appropriate handling and transportation equipment, such as conveyors, vessels, tanks, pipelines, or vehicles to minimize harm due to handling or due to exposure to the environment.

SERVICES

Some services are primarily storage or delivery services. In these instances, the storage or delivery itself is the product offering. This clause can be viewed as an enhancement to the requirements of subclause 7.5.1. Examples include delivery of packages by air freight, trucking services, and food-delivery services.

 # DEFINITIONS

Conformity (3.6.1)—fulfilment of a **requirement** (3.1.2)

NOTE 1   This definition is consistent with ISO/IEC Guide 2 but differs from it in phrasing to fit into the ISO 9000 concepts.
NOTE 2   The term "conformance" is synonymous but deprecated.

Source: ANSI/ISO/ASQ Q9000-2000

 # CONSIDERATIONS FOR DOCUMENTATION

Documentation considerations should include preparation of work instructions needed to ensure proper handling and preservation of product as appropriate.

 # TYPICAL AUDIT ITEMS FOR COMPLIANCE

- Does the organization uniquely identify product during internal processing and delivery?
- Does the organization handle the product during internal processing and delivery so as to preserve conformity to customer requirements?
- Does the organization package the product during internal processing and delivery so as to preserve conformity to requirements?
- Does the organization store the product during internal processing and delivery so as to preserve conformity to requirements?

- Does the organization protect the product during internal processing and delivery so as to preserve conformity to requirements?

7.6 Control of monitoring and measuring devices

The organization shall determine the monitoring and measurement to be undertaken and the monitoring and measuring devices needed to provide evidence of conformity of product to determined requirements (see 7.2.1).

The organization shall establish processes to ensure that monitoring and measurement can be carried out and are carried out in a manner that is consistent with the monitoring and measurement requirements.

Where necessary to ensure valid results, measuring equipment shall

a) be calibrated or verified at specified intervals, or prior to use, against measurement standards traceable to international or national measurement standards; where no such standards exist, the basis used for calibration or verification shall be recorded;

b) be adjusted or re-adjusted as necessary;

c) be identified to enable the calibration status to be determined;

d) be safeguarded from adjustments that would invalidate the measurement result;

e) be protected from damage and deterioration during handling, maintenance and storage.

In addition, the organization shall assess and record the validity of the previous measuring results when the equipment is found not to conform to requirements. The organization shall take appropriate action on the equipment and any product affected. Records of the results of calibration and verification shall be maintained (see 4.2.4).

When used in the monitoring and measurement of specified requirements, the ability of computer software to satisfy the intended application shall be confirmed. This shall be undertaken prior to initial use and reconfirmed as necessary.

NOTE   See ISO 10012-1 and ISO 10012-2 for guidance.

Source: ANSI/ISO/ASQ Q9001-2000

The text from clause 4.11 in ISO 9001:1994 has been reduced and modified. The intent has not been to diminish or increase the level of the requirements. Instead, the change in text is intended to make this section more understandable to providers of software and services.

Measurements must be made to assure that product meets specifications. The necessary measurements need to be identified, along with any special instruments or monitoring and measurement devices needed for making them. This part of the standard is focused on assuring the quality of the measurements and of the monitoring and measurement devices. If the devices used to make measurements are not accurate, are unstable, are damaged in any way, or are inappropriate for making the measurement, then the product may not meet its requirements. Even worse, the organization will not know this. Monitoring and measurement devices need to be capable and their use needs to be controlled.

All monitoring and measurement instruments or equipment required to assure the conformance of product to requirements fall within the scope of this clause.

For both product and process measurements, statistical methods can be useful for demonstrating conformity. This is particularly true for meeting the requirement that the organization must ensure that monitoring and measurement are carried out in a manner that is consistent with the monitoring and measurement requirements. This requirement encompasses two concepts: the concept of achieving and maintaining a capable measurement system (measurement requirements must be met) and the concept of achieving and maintaining a stable measurement system (consistent performance). Statistical methods may be useful for obtaining assurance that this requirement is met.

Monitoring and measurement devices that are required to assure conformity of product need to be controlled. This includes devices used during design and development, those used for inspection and testing of raw materials, those used for in-process and final testing, and those used for monitoring quality once the product has been released to the customer.

The extent of the control to be exercised for the monitoring and measurement devices is listed in items *a* through *e* of clause 7.6 in ISO 9001:2000. Although the concept of a measurement system is not specifically addressed in the standard, clause 7.6 provides the framework for the establishment and maintenance of a measurement system. ISO 10012 is recommended as a reference source for general background and guidance for a measurement system and for the management of monitoring and measurement devices.

When measuring equipment is found not to conform to requirements, the validity of any measurements made since it was last known to be in conformity needs to be investigated. Records of calibrations and verification measurements need to be kept.

SOFTWARE

Software used in monitoring and measurement devices must be appropriate for the type of measurements to be made. This needs to be checked before initial use. Continuing suitability needs to be reconfirmed as necessary.

 DEFINITIONS

Measurement control system (3.10.1)—set of interrelated or interacting elements necessary to achieve **metrological confirmation** (3.10.3) and continual control of **measurement processes** (3.10.2)

Measuring equipment (3.10.4)—measuring instrument, software, measurement standard, reference material or auxiliary apparatus or combination thereof necessary to realize a **measurement process** (3.10.2)

Measurement process (3.10.2)—set of operations to determine the value of a quantity

Source: ANSI/ISO/ASQ Q9000-2000

CONSIDERATIONS FOR DOCUMENTATION

Documentation considerations should include a documented procedure for the control and calibration of monitoring and measurement devices. Work instructions should also be prepared for the actual work of performing the calibrations.

This clause requires records of calibration results with specific reference to clause 4.2.4 for control of the records generated.

TYPICAL AUDIT ITEMS FOR COMPLIANCE

- Has the organization identified the measurements to be made?
- Has the organization identified the monitoring and measurement devices required to assure conformity of product to specified requirements?
- Are monitoring and measurement devices used to ensure measurement capability?
- Are monitoring and measurement devices calibrated and adjusted periodically or before use against devices traceable to international or national standards?
- Is the basis used for calibration recorded when traceability to international or national standards cannot be done, since no standards exist?
- Are monitoring and measurement devices safeguarded from adjustments that would invalidate the calibration?
- Are monitoring and measurement devices protected from damage and deterioration during handling, maintenance, and storage?
- Do monitoring and measurement devices have the results of their calibration recorded?

- Does the organization have the validity of previous results from monitoring and measurement devices reassessed if they are subsequently found to be out of calibration? Is corrective action taken?
- Is the software used for monitoring and measurement of specified requirements confirmed as to its suitability before use?

CHAPTER

9

Measurement

8 Measurement, analysis and improvement

8.1 General

The organization shall plan and implement the monitoring, measurement, analysis and improvement processes needed

a) to demonstrate conformity of the product,

b) to ensure conformity of the quality management system, and

c) to continually improve the effectiveness of the quality management system.

This shall include determination of applicable methods, including statistical techniques, and the extent of their use.

Source: ANSI/ISO/ASQ Q9001-2000

 This clause applies to all product types (hardware, software, and services), to all market sectors, and to organizations of all sizes. Although this clause is only two sentences long, some feel that it is one of the most dramatic clauses in ISO 9001:2000. The other clauses of equal dramatic importance are clause 7.1 and clause 4.1. These three clauses contain the essential requirements of the process model to be used to address product realization, continual improvement, and customer satisfaction.

Clause 8.1 requires organizations to think about the processes used to achieve product realization and to assure that the necessary monitoring, measurement, analysis, and improvement activities are planned and implemented. It is the responsibility of the organization to decide what it needs to monitor and measure, where to monitor and measure, what analyses should be performed, and how the analysis of the data derived from monitoring and measurement should be used. It is worth repeating that the organization decides the "monitoring, measurement, analysis and improvement processes needed to demonstrate conformity of product, to ensure conformity of the quality management system and to continually improve the effectiveness of the quality manage-

ment system." These decisions are not made by external auditors, consultants, the contents of this book, or via interpretations provided by external agencies (for example, by national bodies); rather, they are made by the organization. Herein lies the challenge of ISO 9001:2000. The organization must take ownership of monitoring and measurement of its processes to the extent needed to effectively manage its performance.

Regarding the requirement for determining applicable methodologies, including statistical techniques and the extent of their use, the intent of the new standard is to clarify ISO 9001:1994 to the extent that the use of statistical techniques is a stated requirement. ISO 9004:2000 provides very useful information that should be considered when determining the quality management system requirements for monitoring and measurement activities.

 ## DEFINITIONS

Conformity (3.6.1)—fulfilment of a **requirement** (3.1.2)

NOTE 1   This definition is consistent with ISO/IEC Guide 2 but differs from it in phrasing to fit into the ISO 9000 concepts.

NOTE 2   The term "conformance" is synonymous but deprecated.

Source: ANSI/ISO/ASQ Q9000-2000

 ## CONSIDERATIONS FOR DOCUMENTATION

No specific documentation is advised or necessary to address the requirements of this clause.

 ## TYPICAL AUDIT ITEMS FOR COMPLIANCE

- Is objective evidence available to demonstrate that the organization has defined, planned, and implemented the monitoring and measurement activities needed to assure conformity and to achieve improvement?

- Is objective evidence available to demonstrate that the organization has determined the need for and use of applicable methodologies, including statistical techniques?

8.2 Monitoring and measurement

8.2.1 Customer satisfaction

As one of the measurements of the performance of the quality management system, the organization shall monitor information relating to customer perception as to whether the organization has met customer requirements. The methods for obtaining and using this information shall be determined.

Source: ANSI/ISO/ASQ Q9001-2000

 An often-voiced criticism of ISO 9001 was that it focused on paper and written procedures rather than on assuring the delivery of products that would address customer satisfaction by meeting customer requirements. This view has persisted even though clause 1, *Scope,* of ISO 9001:1994 stated that the requirements of the standard are ". . . aimed primarily at achieving customer satisfaction by preventing nonconformity. . . ." A primary thrust of ISO 9001:2000 is to increase the emphasis on customer satisfaction, which should be a primary reason for the existence of most organizations. Increased emphasis on customer satisfaction was explicitly and clearly identified as a marketplace need in the market research that was performed by ISO before the development of ISO 9001:2000.

During the development of ISO 9001:2000, the issue of how to address customer satisfaction was hotly debated. Many wanted very aggressive measures as requirements. Others wanted no reference to customer satisfaction, in spite of the "voice of the customer." In addition, the auditability of "soft requirements" was a concern. The final resolution of these conflicting viewpoints was language that requires the organization to "monitor information relating to customer perception as to whether the organization has met customer requirements." For regulated products such as medical devices, this involves, at a minimum, the evaluation of product use or misuse and the evaluation of customer complaints.

The approaches that an organization should use to comply with this requirement are not defined. It is the organization's responsibility to decide what information it will monitor and measure. For example, organizations that function in regulated markets may choose to monitor customer reports of product deficiencies. A large automobile manufacturer might measure customer satisfaction as reflected in surveys mailed to new car owners. Service providers may choose to use focus groups to probe customers' perceptions. Software suppliers could monitor reported bugs from field installations. The important point is that the organization decides what to monitor and what methods to use.

It is worthwhile to recognize the order of "monitoring and measurement." Previous drafts of ISO 9001:2000 presented these action verbs in the order "measure and monitor." Now the order of these terms is reversed. Monitoring usually provides less information than measuring. The results of monitoring may indicate a need to gather more information through measuring. An organization might monitor or measure or do both for similar types of data.

A few examples of sources of customer satisfaction information that could be used to meet the requirements of this clause include the following:

- Customer complaints
- Returns
- Warranty information
- Customer-satisfaction studies
- Results from focus group meetings
- Customer tracking studies
- Questionnaires and surveys
- Reports from consumer organizations

- Direct customer communication
- Benchmarking data
- Industry group information
- Trade association information

Although many sources of information about customer satisfaction and dissatisfaction are typically available, this information is often poorly organized and even more poorly used. This requirement of the standard should encourage organizations to better use the "gold mine" of information readily available to them.

The organization also must decide the extent to which its processes go beyond mere conformance to requirements to meet the unstated needs and expectations of customers. This should include price and delivery considerations. It is up to the organization to decide how far to go in this direction, which should be related to the organization's quality policy and objectives.

The standard takes one additional step in the area of customer satisfaction—it includes a requirement that the methods for obtaining and using customer information must be determined. This means that the organization must think about how to gather information and what will be done with the information after it is gathered. Many organizations gather information, and some make an effort to understand what the information means, but few actually do something to improve the organization and its processes. The intent of the standard is to encourage organizations to plan what to gather, to gather the information, to analyze and understand it, and to take appropriate action.

DEFINITIONS

Conformity (3.6.1)—fulfilment of a **requirement** (3.1.2)

NOTE 1   This definition is consistent with ISO/IEC Guide 2 but differs from it in phrasing to fit into the ISO 9000 concepts.

NOTE 2   The term "conformance" is synonymous but deprecated.

Measurement process (3.10.2)—set of operations to determine the value of a quantity

Source: ANSI/ISO/ASQ Q9000-2000

 CONSIDERATIONS FOR DOCUMENTATION

While no specific documented procedure is needed to address this clause, several processes may be needed to address the requirements for customer-satisfaction measurement. Consideration should be given to documentation of what customer information should be gathered, who should gather it, how often it should be gathered, in what form it should be gathered, who will analyze the information, and what will be done with the results of the analysis.

 TYPICAL AUDIT ITEMS FOR COMPLIANCE

Items representing a difference from ISO 9001:1994 have a Δ at the end.

• Is customer satisfaction information monitored? Δ

• Are methods for gathering and using customer information determined and deployed throughout the organization? Δ

8.2.2 Internal audit

The organization shall conduct internal audits at planned intervals to determine whether the quality management system

a) conforms to the planned arrangements (see 7.1), to the requirements of this International Standard and to the quality management system requirements established by the organization, and

b) is effectively implemented and maintained.

An audit programme shall be planned, taking into consideration the status and importance of the processes and areas to be audited, as well as the results of previous audits. The audit criteria, scope, frequency and methods shall be defined. Selection of auditors and conduct of audits shall ensure objectivity and impartiality of the audit process. Auditors shall not audit their own work.

The responsibilities and requirements for planning and conducting audits, and for reporting results and maintaining records (see 4.2.4) shall be defined in a documented procedure.

The management responsible for the area being audited shall ensure that actions are taken without undue delay to eliminate detected nonconformities and their causes. Follow-up activities shall include the verification of the actions taken and the reporting of verification results (see 8.5.2).

NOTE   See ISO 10011-1, ISO 10011-2 and ISO 10011-3 for guidance.

Source: ANSI/ISO/ASQ Q9001-2000

The requirements of clause 8.2.2 have not changed substantively from the 1994 standard. There have been modest changes to reflect improved practices and to clarify the intent of this clause.

It is now clear that audits are to be carried out periodically. Though this was implied before, it was not clearly stated. A one-time set of audits to comply with ISO 9001 in order to obtain registration is not sufficient. As obvious as this is, some argued that periodic audits were not required. It is now clear that a process is required.

 Planning for audits must take into account a number of factors. It is now required that the results of previous audits are among the factors to be considered. In planning for audits, audit scope, frequency, and methodologies must be defined. This detail was not explicit in the earlier standard.

The 1994 standard contained a statement requiring independence of the auditors—that is, "personnel independent of those having direct responsibility for the activity being audited." For some, this created confusion and created a burden as to how to implement internal audits. Some thought that independence required that all auditors needed to be from distant parts of the organization or needed to report to separate senior executives. The intent of the 1994 standard has been clarified by including language that states that "selection of auditors and conduct of audits shall ensure objectivity and impartiality of the audit process" and that internal "auditors shall not audit their own work."

Internal audit of the quality management system is grouped with clauses for monitoring information relating to customer perception as to whether the organization has met customer requirements, and monitoring and measurement of processes and product. The message is clear: Internal auditing is a form of measurement specifically focused on the quality management system.

Even as we recognize internal audit of the quality management system as a form of measurement, it continues to be an essential process to provide confidence in the effective implementation of the quality management system. To better understand the role of internal audit, it is useful to consider its role as complementary to that of two other forms of quality management system evaluation—management review and self-assessment.

When evaluating quality management systems, the following four basic questions should be asked in relation to every process being evaluated:

Audit Questions

- Is the process identified and appropriately described?
- Are responsibilities assigned?
- Are required processes implemented and maintained?
- Is the process effective in achieving the required results?

The collective answers to these questions determine the outcome of the evaluation.

The evaluation of a quality management system can vary in scope, and it typically encompasses the following three major approaches:

- Auditing, an aspect of which is the subject of this section, ISO 9001:2000, clause 8.2.2, *Internal audit*
- Reviewing the quality management system, the subject of ISO 9001:2000, clause 5.6, *Management review*
- Self-assessments, the subject of ISO 9004:2000, clause 8.2.1.5, *Self-assessment*

Audits are used to evaluate the adequacy of quality management system documentation, conformance to quality management system requirements, and the effectiveness of system implementation. The results of audits can be used to identify opportunities for improvement. There is a slight difference in the way ISO 9001:2000 describes the determination of the effectiveness of the quality management system. The 1994 version had auditors determining the system's effectiveness, while the 2000 version requires auditors to determine the effectiveness of implementation. Determination of overall system suitability and effectiveness is left to top management, who use audit results and other data to make that evaluation.

First-party audits are conducted by or on behalf of the organization for internal purposes and can form the basis for an organization's self-declaration of conformity. Second-party audits are conducted by customers of the organization or by other persons on behalf of a customer. Third-party audits are conducted by external independent audit service organizations. Such organizations can verify conformity with requirements such as those of ISO 9001.

One role of top management is to carry out regular, systematic evaluations of the suitability, adequacy, effectiveness, and efficiency of the quality management system with respect to the quality policy and objectives. This review (see ISO 9001:2000, clause 5.6) can include consideration of the need to adapt the quality policy and objectives in response to the changing needs and expectations of interested parties. The review includes determination of the need for actions. Among other sources of information, audit reports are used for review of the quality management system.

An organization's self-assessment (see ISO 9004:2000, clause 8.2.1.5) is a comprehensive and planned review of the organization's activities and results referenced against the quality management system or a model of excellence. The use of self-assessment methodology can provide an overall view of the performance of the organization and the degree of maturity of the quality management system. It can also help to identify areas requiring improvement in the organization and to determine priorities. Such self-assessments typically go beyond auditing to assess conformance to requirements. They look for opportunities for the organization to improve its efficiency and performance.

Internal quality audits must be conducted periodically and should be used to determine conformity to the requirements of ISO 9001:2000 and the degree to which the quality management system has been effectively implemented and maintained. An indicator of problems with the effectiveness of the quality management system is the occurrence of high numbers of customer complaints or of high levels of scrap and rework within the organization. As given in clause 8.2.1, organizations are expected to monitor customers' perceptions. Internal auditors often use this information to identify product realization processes that require further investigation regarding the extent to which they have been effectively implemented and maintained. In a similar fashion, scrap and rework information may be of value for identifying subject areas for internal audits.

Whatever factors and methods are used, internal quality audits may be performed on processes of the quality management system or on the entire system. Whatever approach is used, details need to be established in plans, and quality system processes should be investigated in order of their priority. Previous audit results should be used in developing the prioritization. The scope of each audit should be clear, and the frequency of audits within the audit program and the audit methodology should be identified. Specific requirements related to audit scope and use of prior audit results are new in ISO 9001:2000.

Internal auditors should be qualified as auditors. This is particularly necessary for "guest" auditors, or technical experts from other functions who are used to provide product or process technical expertise to the effort to evaluate effectiveness but who tend to be inexperienced at auditing.

Audit results should be documented in a written report, and records should indicate deficiencies. Target dates should be established for responding to audit findings and organizations should take timely corrective action. Audit results are required to be inputs to management reviews.

Follow-up actions should be evaluated to assure the effectiveness of the corrective actions.

 DEFINITIONS

Audit (3.9.1)—systematic, independent and documented **process** (3.4.1) for obtaining **audit evidence** (3.9.4) and evaluating it objectively to determine the extent to which **audit criteria** (3.9.3) are fulfilled

NOTE   Internal audits, sometimes called first-party audits, are conducted by, or on behalf of, the **organization** (3.3.1) itself for internal purposes and can form the basis for an organization's self-declaration of **conformity** (3.6.1).

External audits include what are generally termed "second-" or "third-party audits".

Second-party audits are conducted by parties having an interest in the organization, such as customers, or by other persons on their behalf.

Third-party audits are conducted by external independent organizations. Such organizations provide certification or registration of conformity with requirements such as those of ISO 9001 and ISO 14001:1996.

When quality and environmental **management systems** (3.2.2) are audited together, this is termed a "combined audit".

When two or more auditing organizations cooperate to audit a single **auditee** (3.9.8) jointly, this is termed "joint audit".

Audit client (3.9.7)—**organization** (3.3.1) or person requesting an **audit** (3.9.1)

Audit conclusion (3.9.6)—outcome of an **audit** (3.9.1) provided by the **audit team** (3.9.10) after consideration of the audit objectives and all **audit findings** (3.9.5)

Audit criteria (3.9.3) set of policies, **procedures** (3.4.5) or **requirements** (3.1.2) used as a reference

Auditee (3.9.8)—**organization** (3.3.1) being audited

Audit evidence (3.9.4)—**records** (3.7.6), statements of fact or other **information** (3.7.1)—which are relevant to the **audit criteria** (3.9.3) and verifiable

NOTE   Audit evidence can be qualitative or quantitative.

Audit findings (3.9.5)—results of the evaluation of the collected **audit evidence** (3.9.4) against **audit criteria** (3.9.3)

NOTE   Audit findings can indicate either conformity or nonconformity with audit criteria, or opportunities for improvement.

Audit programme (3.9.2)—set of one or more **audits** (3.9.1) planned for a specific time frame and directed towards a specific purpose

Audit team (3.9.10)—one or more **auditors** (3.9.9) conducting an **audit** (3.9.1)

NOTE 1   One auditor in the audit team is generally appointed as audit team leader.

NOTE 2   The audit team can include auditors-in-training and, where required, **technical experts** (3.9.11).

NOTE 3   Observers can accompany the audit team but do not act as part of it.

Auditor (3.9.9)—person with the **competence** (3.9.12) to conduct an **audit** (3.9.1)

Corrective action (3.6.5)—action to eliminate the cause of a detected **nonconformity** (3.6.2) or other undesirable situation

NOTE 1   There can be more than one cause for a nonconformity.

NOTE 2   Corrective action is taken to prevent recurrence whereas **preventive action** (3.6.4) is taken to prevent occurrence.

NOTE 3   There is a distinction between **correction** (3.6.6) and corrective action.

Management (3.2.6)—coordinated activities to direct and control an **organization** (3.3.1)

NOTE   In English, the term "management" sometimes refers to people, i.e. a person or group of people with authority and responsibility for the conduct and control of an organization. When "management" is used in this sense it should always be used with some form of qualifier to avoid confusion with the concept "management" defined above. For example, "management shall" is deprecated whereas "**top management** (3.2.7) shall" is acceptable.

Procedure (3.4.5)—specified way to carry out an activity or a **process** (3.4.1)

NOTE 1   Procedures can be documented or not.

NOTE 2   When a procedure is documented, the term "written procedure" or "documented procedure" is frequently used. The **document** (3.7.2) that contains a procedure can be called a "procedure document".

Record (3.7.6)—**document** (3.7.2) stating results achieved or providing evidence of activities performed

NOTE 1   Records can be used, for example, to document **traceability** (3.5.4) and to provide evidence of **verification** (3.8.4), **preventive action** (3.6.4) and **corrective action** (3.6.5).

NOTE 2   Generally records need not be under revision control.

Technical expert (3.9.11)—person who provides specific knowledge of or expertise on the subject to be audited

NOTE 1   Specific knowledge or expertise includes knowledge of or expertise on the **organization** (3.3.1), **process** (3.4.1) or activity to be audited, as well as language or cultural guidance.

Verification (3.8.4)—confirmation, through the provision of **objective evidence** (3.8.1), that specified **requirements** (3.1.2) have been fulfilled

NOTE 1   The term "verified" is used to designate the corresponding status.

NOTE 2   Confirmation can comprise activities such as

—performing alternative calculations,

—comparing a new design **specification** (3.7.3) with a similar proven design specification,

—undertaking **tests** (3.8.3) and demonstrations, and

—reviewing documents prior to issue.

Source: ANSI/ISO/ASQ Q9000-2000

CONSIDERATIONS FOR DOCUMENTATION

A documented procedure is required that describes the responsibilities and requirements for conducting audits, for ensuring the independence of the audits, for recording results, and for reporting the audit results.

This clause also does not require any specific records. The planning for realization processes covered in clause 7.1 should define the records the organization will keep. It would usually be expected of the organization to have records of audit plans and descriptions of audits, including their scope, frequency, and methodologies used. Records should be available to provide evidence that audit findings were reported and that there was timely corrective action on deficiencies found during the audit. There should also be records that verification was performed for the implementation of corrective action and that the verification results were reported.

TYPICAL AUDIT ITEMS FOR COMPLIANCE

- Does the organization conduct periodic audits of the quality management system?
- Do the periodic audits evaluate the conformity of the quality management system to the requirements of ISO 9001:2000?
- Do the periodic audits evaluate the degree to which the quality management system has been effectively implemented and maintained?
- Does the organization plan the audit program taking into consideration the status and importance of areas to be audited?
- Does the organization plan the audit program taking into consideration the results of previous audits? Δ
- Are the audit scope, frequency, and methodologies defined? Δ

- Does the audit process and auditor assignment ensure objectivity and impartiality? Δ
- Is there a documented procedure that includes the responsibilities and requirements for conducting audits?
- Is there a documented procedure that describes how to ensure the independence of auditors?
- Is there a documented procedure for reporting results and maintaining records?
- Is timely corrective action taken on deficiencies found during the audit?
- Do follow-up actions include the verification of the implementation of corrective action?
- Do follow-up actions include the reporting of verification results?

8.2.3 Monitoring and measurement of processes

The organization shall apply suitable methods for monitoring and, where applicable, measurement of the quality management system processes. These methods shall demonstrate the ability of the processes to achieve planned results. When planned results are not achieved, correction and corrective action shall be taken, as appropriate, to ensure conformity of the product.

Source: ANSI/ISO/ASQ Q9001-2000

  Clause 8.2.3 contains new requirements. These requirements go beyond those of clause 4.9, *Process control,* in ISO 9001:1994, which required "monitoring and control of suitable process parameters and product characteristics." The monitoring and measurement activities of ISO 9001:2000 apply to all relevant processes of the quality management system, not just those that deal with product realization.

These are broad requirements. Early drafts of ISO 9001:2000 limited the scope of process monitoring and measuring to just the product realization processes. There was considerable debate about the extension of this clause to include all processes of the quality management system. It was decided that the most important processes that affect the organization's output need to be covered by this clause. Each organization must determine, plan, and implement the monitoring and measurement activities needed to achieve the planned results of all quality management system processes. This includes, as appropriate, the processes of management responsibility, the resource processes, the measurement and improvement processes, and the product realization processes.

Realistically, not all processes or all process parameters can be monitored or measured. The number of even the most basic processes and process parameters that are candidates for monitoring can be overwhelming. Clause 8.4, *Analysis of data,* of ISO 9001:2000 can be a valuable source of information in identifying the key processes to monitor and the measurements needed to ensure conformity of product. It encompasses the use of applicable methodologies, including statistical techniques for determining what to measure. Data from capability studies commonly are used to help determine what processes have high inherent variation and require tight control versus what processes are both capable and relatively stable.

Clause 8.2.3 links to 8.5.2, *Corrective action.* When process monitoring or measurements indicate that the desired results are not being achieved, then the process needs correction. If appropriate, corrective action needs to be performed to identify and eliminate root causes.

DEFINITIONS

Measurement process (3.10.2)—set of operations to determine the value of a quantity

Process (3.4.1)—set of interrelated or interacting activities which transforms inputs into outputs

NOTE 1   Inputs to a process are generally outputs of other processes.

NOTE 2   Processes in an **organization** (3.3.1) are generally planned and carried out under controlled conditions to add value.

NOTE 3   A process where the **conformity** (3.6.1) of the resulting **product** (3.4.2) cannot be readily or economically verified is frequently referred to as a "special process".

Record (3.7.6)—**document** (3.7.2) stating results achieved or providing evidence of activities performed

NOTE 1   Records can be used, for example, to document **traceability** (3.5.4) and to provide evidence of **verification** (3.8.4), **preventive action** (3.6.4) and **corrective action** (3.6.5).

NOTE 2   Generally records need not be under revision control.

Requirement (3.1.2)—need or expectation that is stated, generally implied or obligatory

NOTE 1   "Generally implied" means that it is custom or common practice for the **organization** (3.3.1), its **customers** (3.3.5) and other **interested parties** (3.3.7), that the need or expectation under consideration is implied.

NOTE 2   A qualifier can be used to denote a specific type of requirement, e.g. product requirement, quality management requirement, customer requirement.

NOTE 3   A specified requirement is one which is stated, for example, in a **document** (3.7.2).

NOTE 4   Requirements can be generated by different interested parties.

Source: ANSI/ISO/ASQ Q9000-2000

CONSIDERATIONS FOR DOCUMENTATION

Objective evidence confirming the effective operation and control of processes for monitoring and measuring all processes needs to be available. This will vary depending upon the size and type of organization, the complexity and interaction of processes, and the competence of personnel. Objective evidence may be in the form of documented procedures and documented records, particularly where manual measurement processes are used. This may be demonstrated through observation of these monitoring and measurement processes, particularly when online sensors and electro-mechanical, closed-loop feedback systems are employed.

TYPICAL AUDIT ITEMS FOR COMPLIANCE

- Have the key quality management system processes, especially the product realization processes, needed to meet planned results been identified? Δ

- Are suitable methods used to measure and monitor these key processes?

- Are the intended purposes of the key processes quantified by process parameter specifications, by specifications for the product output of the process, or by some other means?

- Are the monitoring and measurement methods for processes of the quality management system adequate for confirming the continuing suitability of each process to satisfy its intended purpose and achieve its planned result?

8.2.4 Monitoring and measurement of product

The organization shall monitor and measure the characteristics of the product to verify that product requirements have been met. This shall be carried out at appropriate stages of the product realization process in accordance with the planned arrangements (see 7.1).

Evidence of conformity with the acceptance criteria shall be maintained. Records shall indicate the person(s) authorizing release of product (see 4.2.4).

Product release and service delivery shall not proceed until the planned arrangements (see 7.1) have been satisfactorily completed, unless otherwise approved by a relevant authority and, where applicable, by the customer.

Source: ANSI/ISO/ASQ Q9001-2000

The requirements of ISO 9001:1994 for monitoring and measuring product have not significantly changed. Unlike the previous clause on process measurement, this is not a new requirement. In fact, it is a simplification of ISO 9001:1994, clause 4.10, *Inspection and testing*. The requirements for monitoring and measuring of product, whether they are for software, hardware, processed material, or a service, are all now stated in this generic clause. The previous standard was criticized because the text of clause 4.10 was not in generic language. For example, a service provider had tremendous difficulty in understanding what was meant by "release under positive-recall procedures shall not preclude the activities outlined in . . ." (ISO 9001:1994, clause 4.10.3). The generic nature of the current text is not intended to soften the requirement to measure and monitor the characteristics of the product to verify that requirements for the product are met.

The scope of this clause includes all measurement activities associated with materials, components, assemblies, and product from receiving inspection to product delivery. It covers the actual measurements used to verify that requirements are met for the materials that go into the product as well as the product itself at appropriate stages of the product-realization process.

For purchased material, clause 7.4.3, *Verification of purchased product,* from ISO 9001:2000 requires the organization to identify and implement verification activities. The requirements for the associated measures are contained here, in ISO 9001:2000, clause 8.2.4, *monitoring and measurement of product.*

For in-process and final product, clause 7.5.1, *Operations control,* from ISO 9001:2000 requires the organization to implement defined processes for monitoring, measurement, release, and delivery.

Conformity to requirements needs to be documented. Records need to indicate who within the organization has the authority to release final product. Analysis of the data for release and also for improvement is detailed in ISO 9001:2000, clause 8.4, *Analysis of data.* This includes the use of applicable methodologies, including statistical techniques to determine the type of data to collect and the decision rules for release.

Product release and service delivery require that all specified activities be accomplished unless release is otherwise approved by a relevant authority or by the customer. This usually means that some form of record is available to document that specified activities have been accomplished.

DEFINITIONS

Characteristic (3.5.1)—distinguishing feature

NOTE 1   A characteristic can be inherent or assigned.

NOTE 2   A characteristic can be qualitative or quantitative.

NOTE 3   There are various classes of characteristic, such as the following:

—physical (e.g. mechanical, electrical, chemical or biological characteristics);

—sensory (e.g. related to smell, touch, taste, sight, hearing);

—behavioral (e.g. courtesy, honesty, veracity);

—temporal (e.g. punctuality, reliability, availability);

—ergonomic (e.g. physiological characteristic, or related to human safety);

—functional (e.g. maximum speed of an aircraft).

Measurement process (3.10.2)—set of operations to determine the value of a quantity

Objective evidence (3.8.1)—data supporting the existence or verity of something

NOTE   Objective evidence may be obtained through observation, measurement, **test** (3.8.3), or other means.

Product (3.4.2)—result of a **process** (3.4.1)

NOTE 1   There are four generic product categories, as follows:

—services (e.g. transport);

—software (e.g. computer program, dictionary);

—hardware (e.g. engine mechanical part);

—processed materials (e.g. lubricant).

Many products comprise elements belonging to different generic product categories. Whether the product is then called service, software, hardware or processed material depends on the dominant element. For example the offered product "automobile" consists of hardware (e.g. tyres), processed materials (e.g. fuel, cooling liquid), software (e.g. engine control software, driver's manual), and service (e.g. operating explanations given by the salesman).

NOTE 2   Service is the result of at least one activity necessarily performed at the interface between the **supplier** (3.3.6) and **customer** (3.3.5) and is generally intangible. Provision of a service can involve, for example, the following:

—an activity performed on a customer-supplied tangible product (e.g. automobile to be repaired);

—an activity performed on a customer-supplied intangible product (e.g. the income statement needed to prepare a tax return);

—the delivery of an intangible product (e.g. the delivery of information in the context of knowledge transmission);

—the creation of ambience for the customer (e.g. in hotels and restaurants).

Software consists of information and is generally intangible and can be in the form of approaches, transactions or **procedures** (3.4.5).

Hardware is generally tangible and its amount is a countable **characteristic** (3.5.1). Processed materials are generally tangible and their amount is a continuous characteristic. Hardware and processed materials often are referred to as goods.

NOTE 3   **Quality assurance** (3.2.11) is mainly focused on intended product.

Quality characteristic (3.5.2)—inherent **characteristic** (3.5.1) of a **product** (3.4.2), **process** (3.4.1) or **system** (3.2.1) related to a **requirement** (3.1.2)

NOTE 1   Inherent means existing in something, especially as a permanent characteristic.

NOTE 2   A characteristic assigned to a product, process or system (e.g. the price of a product, the owner of a product) is not a quality characteristic of that product, process or system.

Requirement (3.1.2)—need or expectation that is stated, generally implied or obligatory

NOTE 1   "Generally implied" means that it is custom or common practice for the **organization** (3.3.1), its **customers** (3.3.5) and other **interested parties** (3.3.7), that the need or expectation under consideration is implied.

NOTE 2   A qualifier can be used to denote a specific type of requirement, e.g. product requirement, quality management requirement, customer requirement.

NOTE 3   A specified requirement is one which is stated, for example, in a **document** (3.7.2).

NOTE 4   Requirements can be generated by different interested parties.

Source: ANSI/ISO/ASQ Q9000-2000

 # CONSIDERATIONS FOR DOCUMENTATION

Consideration should be given to the work instructions needed to ensure that measurement of product is conducted as planned. Records are required to provide objective evidence that the product acceptance criteria have been met. They should also indicate the authority responsible for release of the product. This clause contains specific reference to clause 5.5.7 for control of the records generated.

TYPICAL AUDIT ITEMS FOR COMPLIANCE

- Does the organization measure and monitor product characteristics to verify that product requirements are met?
- Does the organization measure and monitor product characteristics at appropriate stages of the product realization process?
- Is there objective evidence that acceptance criteria for product have been met?
- Do records identify the person authorizing release of the product?
- Are all specified activities performed before product release and service delivery?
- If there are instances in which all specified activities have not been performed before product release or service delivery, has a relevant authority, or as appropriate the customer, been informed and approved of the action?

CHAPTER

10

Control of Nonconforming Product

8.3 Control of nonconforming product

The organization shall ensure that product which does not conform to product requirements is identified and controlled to prevent its unintended use or delivery. The controls and related responsibilities and authorities for dealing with nonconforming product shall be defined in a documented procedure.

The organization shall deal with nonconforming product by one or more of the following ways:

a) by taking action to eliminate the detected nonconformity;

b) by authorizing its use, release or acceptance under concession by a relevant authority and, where applicable, by the customer;

c) by taking action to preclude its original intended use or application.

Records of the nature of nonconformities and any subsequent actions taken, including concessions obtained, shall be maintained (see 4.2.4).

When nonconforming product is corrected it shall be subject to re-verification to demonstrate conformity to the requirements.

When nonconforming product is detected after delivery or use has started, the organization shall take action appropriate to the effects, or potential effects, of the nonconformity.

Source: ANSI/ISO/ASQ Q9001-2000

The content of clause 8.3 is consistent with the requirements contained in ISO 9001:1994. A great deal of flexibility is given to the organization in the implementation of processes to control nonconformities.

A primary requirement of clause 8.3 is to assure the effective implementation of processes that prevent unintended use or delivery of product that does not conform to requirements. This is a simple requirement that makes business sense. The challenge to an organization is to devise processes that provide a high degree of assurance that this objective is accomplished. There should be a robust approach for identifying, controlling, and preventing unintended use of such product.

Documented procedures are required for detailing the controls and for making clear who is responsible for dealing with the nonconforming product. Typically, organizations will establish processes that provide for review of nonconformity by appropriate individuals in the organization. Such processes may have different levels of approval, depending on the nature of the decision regarding the action to be taken for the nonconformity.

The organization has a number of options for dispositioning nonconforming material. It may be scrapped, reworked, repaired or regraded, or for purchased material, it may be returned to a supplier. When the nonconforming product is corrected, conformance to the original requirements needs to be verified.

Often, organizations will not correct nonconforming product. Products that meet functional requirements are often used as is, without action being taken to make the product fully conform with all requirements, especially if such a decision will not affect the conformance of the end product ultimately delivered to a customer. A decision to "use as is," for example, may require engineering approval, while manufacturing management may be permitted to approve a rework or scrap disposition of a nonconformity.

It may be required (for example, by contract or by internal procedures) to report a proposed rectification of nonconforming product for concession to the customer, the end user, a regulatory body, or any other body. In such cases the organization should have processes in place to assure that such reporting to the customer occurs.

There are specific requirements for records of nonconforming product. Organizations should maintain records of the nonconformities, the action taken to resolve them, and any required internal or external approvals.

This clause also requires the organization to take appropriate action when the organization delivers product that is subsequently determined to be nonconforming. Although it is not explicitly stated, records of such action should be maintained, if only to document the use of prudent judgment in addressing such situations.

DEFINITIONS

Concession (3.6.11)—permission to use or release a **product** (3.4.2) that does not conform to specified **requirements** (3.1.2)

NOTE   A concession is generally limited to the delivery of a product that has nonconforming **characteristics** (3.5.1) within specified limits for an agreed time or quantity of that product.

Conformity (3.6.1)—fulfilment of a **requirement** (3.1.2)

NOTE 1   This definition is consistent with ISO/IEC Guide 2 but differs from it in phrasing to fit into the ISO 9000 concepts.

NOTE 2   The term "conformance" is synonymous but deprecated.

Correction (3.6.6)—action to eliminate a detected **nonconformity** (3.6.2)

NOTE 1   A correction can be made in conjunction with a **corrective action** (3.6.5).

NOTE 2   A correction can be, for example, **rework** (3.6.7) or **regrade** (3.6.8).

Defect (3.6.3)—non-fulfilment of a **requirement** (3.1.2) related to an intended or specified use

NOTE 1   The distinction between the concepts defect and **nonconformity** (3.6.2) is important as it has legal connotations, particularly those associated with product liability issues. Consequently the term "defect" should be used with extreme caution.

NOTE 2   The intended use as intended by the **customer** (3.3.5) can be affected by the nature of the information, such as operating or maintenance instructions, provided by the **supplier** (3.3.6).

Nonconformity (3.6.2)—non-fulfilment of a **requirement** (3.1.2)

Regrade (3.6.8)—alteration of the **grade** (3.1.3) of a nonconforming **product** (3.4.2) in order to make it conform to **requirements** (3.1.2) differing from the initial ones

Release (3.6.13)—permission to proceed to the next stage of a **process** (3.4.1)

NOTE   In English, in the context of computer software, the term "release" is frequently used to refer to a version of the software itself.

Repair (3.6.9)—action on a nonconforming **product** (3.4.2) to make it acceptable for the intended use

NOTE 1   Repair includes remedial action taken on a previously conforming product to restore it for use, for example as part of maintenance.

NOTE 2   Unlike **rework** (3.6.7), repair can affect or change parts of the nonconforming product.

Rework (3.6.7)—action on a nonconforming **product** (3.4.2) to make it conform to the **requirements** (3.1.2)

NOTE   Unlike rework, **repair** (3.6.9) can affect or change parts of the nonconforming product.

Scrap (3.6.10)—action on a nonconforming **product** (3.4.2) to preclude its originally intended use

EXAMPLE   Recycling, destruction.

NOTE   In a nonconforming service situation, use is precluded by discontinuing the service.

Source: ANSI/ISO/ASQ Q9000-2000

CONSIDERATIONS FOR DOCUMENTATION

A documented procedure is required to ensure that product that does not conform to requirements is identified and controlled to prevent unintended use or delivery. The organization should consider documenting a process for addressing the disposition of nonconforming product and, where appropriate, reverifying the product. This documentation could be a separate procedure or a part of a comprehensive nonconformity procedure.

The organization should also consider preparing a documented procedure to address situations in which nonconforming product is detected after delivery to or use by a customer has occurred. Finally, documented procedures should describe communications with customers, where appropriate, of circumstances that involve proposed rectification of product nonconformity should be considered. This documentation could be in the form of separate procedures or a part of a comprehensive nonconformity procedure.

TYPICAL AUDIT ITEMS FOR COMPLIANCE

- Is there a documented procedure to assure that product that does not conform to requirements is identified and controlled to prevent unintended use or delivery?

- Is there evidence of appropriate action being taken when nonconforming product has been detected after delivery or use has started?
- Is it required that any proposed rectification of nonconforming product be reported for concession to the customer, the end-user, or a regulatory body?
- Is there objective evidence of appropriate communication with a customer when the organization proposes rectification of nonconforming product?
- Are concessions obtained from customers as appropriate?

CHAPTER

11

Analysis of Data

> ## 8.4 Analysis of data
>
> The organization shall determine, collect and analyse appropriate data to demonstrate the suitability and effectiveness of the quality management system and to evaluate where continual improvement of the effectiveness of the quality management system can be made. This shall include data generated as a result of monitoring and measurement and from other relevant sources.
>
> The analysis of data shall provide information relating to
>
> a) customer satisfaction (see 8.2.1),
>
> b) conformity to product requirements (see 7.2.1),
>
> c) characteristics and trends of processes and products including opportunities for preventive action, and
>
> d) suppliers.

Source: ANSI/ISO/ASQ Q9001-2000

For analysis of data, clause 4.14.3a of ISO 9001:1994 only requires that certain sources of information be used to " . . . detect, analyze, and eliminate potential causes of nonconformities. . . ." With the exception of this clause, ISO 9001:1994 is silent on the concept of analysis.

 ISO 9001:2000 goes beyond the ISO 9001:1994 requirement to use analysis in the preventive action process to eliminate potential causes of nonconformity. It states the following two purposes for analyzing data:

• To determine the suitability and effectiveness of the quality management system

• To identify improvements that can be made to quality management system effectiveness

The organization must determine what data to collect and collect it. But collection of data without developing the data into useful information is a waste of organizational resources. It must analyze data. One of the most important considerations in establishing data collection methods is to determine how the data will be used. When a data collection scheme has been well designed, the analysis effort is minimized. Data collection systems that are poorly designed may not only be inefficient, but may also yield incorrect information.

An organization dedicated to continual improvement will view the requirements of clauses 5, 6, 7, and 8 as linked in the sense that the organization should function on a closed-loop basis. This means continually measuring processes and products, analyzing data, and improving the system.

Information from the analysis of data should be used as part of the management review input. Analysis may also be conducted as a part of the management review itself. Clause 8.4 requires analysis to determine the suitability and effectiveness of the quality management system, and clause 5.6.1 requires that top management review the quality management system to ensure its suitability, adequacy, and effectiveness. Top management has a good deal of flexibility in complying with these requirements. Options for top management include the following:

- Data may be analyzed "off line," and information from the analysis may be provided as input to top management for use in determining the suitability and effectiveness of the system. This may be typical of larger organizations or organizations with dedicated analytical staff.
- The data may be provided to top management; in this case, top managers would conduct the analysis as a part of the management review. This may be more typical for a small organization.

The organization is required to analyze data to identify areas where improvements can be made. The analysis must provide information in four specific areas: customer satisfaction; conformance to product requirements; characteristics of processes, product and their trends; and suppliers. The specific information that is appropriate may differ based on the type and size of the organization as well as on the product category.

Customer-related information is different from the information related to meeting product requirements. It is possible for customers to be satisfied with product that is nonconforming or to be highly dissatisfied with product that fully conforms with requirements. In either case, identifying the causes of customer dissatisfaction offers an opportunity to change requirements to reflect actual customer needs. The customer information monitored must relate to customer perceptions and may include such items as issues of importance to customers, gaps in meeting customer expectations, customers' desires for changes in the product characteristics, the relative satisfaction of customers with the organization and its competitors, or customer complaints.

The appropriate information on customer satisfaction may depend upon the nature of an organization's relationships with its customers. For example, large organizations selling products to consumers through multiple distribution channels may need information about several tiers of customers in their value chains. This may include information on both the various distribution channels and consumers. This could be the case for toy manufacturers (hardware), home computer software providers (software), and airlines (service). At the other extreme, organizations with a single customer and day-to-day personal customer contact may have significantly different information needs.

Information about conformance to product requirements includes information that describes how well the customer's requirements are being met. It may include information on those requirements the organization has derived from needs and expectations not specifically stated by the customer. This is very different from information about customer perceptions. Inspections and test results, field problem reports, and warranty returns are typical of data related to conformance to requirements.

Information on characteristics of processes, products, and their trends can be derived from analyses of product and process data obtained from the measurement process. This may also include information from aggregation and analysis of both internal operational data and feedback from customers.

Information on suppliers can be obtained from analyses of supplier performance data. It may include information on both excellent and poorly performing suppliers. Since purchased material is often a significant percentage of the total cost of goods sold, it makes business sense to invest appropriately in assuring excellent performance by suppliers (for example, zero defects or 100 percent on-time delivery).

HARDWARE AND PROCESSED MATERIALS

Information about conformance to product requirements in this category may include such items as the most numerous and significant nonconformities reported by the customer, the costs of customer returns, and significant design changes resulting from customer feedback. Information on characteristics of processes, products, and their trends may include the capabilities of manufacturing processes, types of significant assembly defects, order entry error rates, and statistical process control data. It may also include such items as line balance information, cell cycle times, and other information needed to improve scheduling and cycle time.

SERVICES

Information about conformance to service product requirements may include such items as significant nonconformities to customer requirements by customer-contact employees or service deliverers. The information may also include causes of late service performance, the most significant reasons for service outages, opportunities to reduce unavailability of service due to overcapacity scheduling, inadequate documentation, billing, and other accounting errors.

Information on the characteristics of processes, products, and their trends may include significant causes of process backlogs, the ability of key service processes to deliver required services when requested by the customer, the time needed to respond to service requests, satisfaction with delivered training, the acceptability of consulting services, the late delivery of services, and late or over-budget development projects.

SOFTWARE

Information about conformance to software product requirements may include such items as the most numerous or most significant nonconformities reported by the customer, the cost to correct a nonconformity, and issues related to installation and start-up.

Information on the characteristics of processes, products, and their trends may include rates of decline of bugs found, percentage of on-time releases, the acceptability of design and development reviews, and controlling change.

 DEFINITIONS

Characteristic (3.5.1)—distinguishing feature

NOTE 1   A characteristic can be inherent or assigned.
NOTE 2   A characteristic can be qualitative or quantitative.
NOTE 3   There are various classes of characteristic, such as the following:
—physical (e.g. mechanical, electrical, chemical or biological characteristics);
—sensory (e.g. related to smell, touch, taste, sight, hearing);
—behavioral (e.g. courtesy, honesty, veracity);
—temporal (e.g. punctuality, reliability, availability);
—ergonomic (e.g. physiological characteristic, or related to human safety);
—functional (e.g. maximum speed of an aircraft).

Customer (3.3.5)—**organization** (3.3.1) or person that receives a **product** (3.4.2)

EXAMPLE   Consumer, client, end-user, retailer, beneficiary and purchaser.
NOTE   A customer can be internal or external to the organization.

Customer satisfaction (3.1.4)—customer's perception of the degree to which the customer's **requirements** (3.1.2) have been fulfilled

NOTE 1   Customer complaints are a common indicator of low customer satisfaction but their absence does not necessarily imply high customer satisfaction.
NOTE 2   Even when customer requirements have been agreed with the customer and fulfilled, this does not necessarily ensure high customer satisfaction.

Effectiveness (3.2.14)—extent to which planned activities are realized and planned results achieved

Management system (3.2.2)—**system** (3.2.1) to establish policy and objectives and to achieve those objectives

NOTE   A management system of an **organization** (3.3.1) can include different management systems, such as a **quality management system** (3.2.3), a financial management system or an environmental management system.

Measurement process (3.10.2)—set of operations to determine the value of a quantity

Process (3.4.1)—set of interrelated or interacting activities which transforms inputs into outputs

NOTE 1   Inputs to a process are generally outputs of other processes.

NOTE 2   Processes in an **organization** (3.3.1) are generally planned and carried out under controlled conditions to add value.

NOTE 3   A process where the **conformity** (3.6.1) of the resulting **product** (3.4.2) cannot be readily or economically verified is frequently referred to as a "special process".

Product (3.4.2)—result of a **process** (3.4.1)

NOTE 1   There are four generic product categories, as follows:

—services (e.g. transport);

—software (e.g. computer program, dictionary);

—hardware (e.g. engine mechanical part);

—processed materials (e.g. lubricant).

Many products comprise elements belonging to different generic product categories. Whether the product is then called service, software, hardware or processed material depends on the dominant element. For example the offered product "automobile" consists of hardware (e.g. tyres), processed materials (e.g. fuel, cooling liquid), software (e.g. engine control software, driver's manual), and service (e.g. operating explanations given by the salesman).

NOTE 2   Service is the result of at least one activity necessarily performed at the interface between the **supplier** (3.3.6) and **customer** (3.3.5) and is generally intangible. Provision of a service can involve, for example, the following:

—an activity performed on a customer-supplied tangible product (e.g. automobile to be repaired);

—an activity performed on a customer-supplied intangible product (e.g. the income statement needed to prepare a tax return);

—the delivery of an intangible product (e.g. the delivery of information in the context of knowledge transmission);

—the creation of ambience for the customer (e.g. in hotels and restaurants).

Software consists of information and is generally intangible and can be in the form of approaches, transactions or **procedures** (3.4.5).

Hardware is generally tangible and its amount is a countable **characteristic** (3.5.1). Processed materials are generally tangible and their amount is a continuous characteristic. Hardware and processed materials often are referred to as goods.

NOTE 3   **Quality assurance** (3.2.11) is mainly focused on intended product.

Quality characteristic (3.5.2)—inherent **characteristic** (3.5.1) of a **product** (3.4.2), **process** (3.4.1) or **system** (3.2.1) related to a **requirement** (3.1.2)

NOTE 1   Inherent means existing in something, especially as a permanent characteristic.

NOTE 2   A characteristic assigned to a product, process or system (e.g. the price of a product, the owner of a product) is not a quality characteristic of that product, process or system.

Requirement (3.1.2)—need or expectation that is stated, generally implied or obligatory

NOTE 1   "Generally implied" means that it is custom or common practice for the **organization** (3.3.1), its **customers** (3.3.5) and other **interested parties** (3.3.7), that the need or expectation under consideration is implied.

NOTE 2   A qualifier can be used to denote a specific type of requirement, e.g. product requirement, quality management requirement, customer requirement.

NOTE 3   A specified requirement is one which is stated, for example, in a **document** (3.7.2).

NOTE 4   Requirements can be generated by different interested parties.

Source: ANSI/ISO/ASQ Q9000-2000

 ## TYPICAL AUDIT ITEMS FOR COMPLIANCE

Items representing a difference from ISO 9001:1994 have a Δ at the end.

- Has the organization determined the appropriate data to be collected?
- Does the organization analyze the appropriate data to determine the suitability and effectiveness of the quality management system? Δ
- Does the organization analyze appropriate data to identify improvements that can be made? Δ
- Does the organization analyze appropriate data to provide information on customer satisfaction? Δ

- Does the organization analyze appropriate data to provide information on conformance to product requirements? Δ
- Does the organization analyze appropriate data to provide information on characteristics of processes, products, and their trends? Δ
- Does the organization analyze appropriate data to provide information on suppliers? Δ

CHAPTER

12

Improvement

8.5 Improvement

8.5.1 Continual improvement

The organization shall continually improve the effectiveness of the quality management system through the use of the quality policy, quality objectives, audit results, analysis of data, corrective and preventive actions and management review.

Source: ANSI/ISO/ASQ Q9001-2000

The key requirements for continual improvement in this standard were in ISO 9001:1994 with the exception of data analysis (which was implied but not explicitly stated as a requirement). Many practitioners argued that ISO 9001:1994 did not deal with continual improvement because there was not a separate section titled as such. To end this debate and to clearly communicate the mechanism for achieving an important quality principle, clause 8.5 was created and titled *Improvement.*

 ISO 9001:2000 makes it clear that continual improvement must be planned and implemented (see 8.1). The key elements for continual improvement are listed in 8.5.1 and are identified as constituting the major items that, working together, serve as the primary means of continually improving the effectiveness of the quality management system.

While clause 8.5 contains the requirements for corrective and preventive actions, the other key elements for improvement of the quality management system are located elsewhere in the standard. To be even clearer about what is expected of organizations, the requirement now is that the quality policy must include a commitment to continual improvement. Clause 5.3b requires that the policy include ". . . commitment to . . . continual improvement." Objectives must be used as an element of continual improvement. The setting of objectives consistent with a quality policy containing a commitment to continual improvement is required in clause 5.4.1. This is also discussed in chapter 3. Audit results form a key input in determining where opportunities lie for continual improvement.

As discussed in chapter 11, the analysis of data must be performed to provide information for identifying opportunities for improvement. Management reviews required by clause 5.6 provide a mechanism to ensure that top management reviews the status of corrective and preventive actions and acts to improve the quality management system and its processes.

SERVICES, HARDWARE, PROCESSED MATERIALS, AND SOFTWARE

The practices required to comply with the general management clauses are essentially identical regardless of the category of product.

 DEFINITIONS

Continual improvement (3.2.13)—recurring activity to increase the ability to fulfil **requirements** (3.1.2)

NOTE   The **process** (3.4.1) of establishing objectives and finding opportunities for improvement is a continual process through the use of **audit findings** (3.9.5) and **audit conclusions** (3.9.6), analysis of data, management **reviews** (3.8.7) or other means and generally leads to **corrective action** (3.6.5) or **preventive action** (3.6.4).

Organization (3.3.1)—group of people and facilities with an arrangement of responsibilities, authorities and relationships

EXAMPLE   Company, corporation, firm, enterprise, institution, charity, sole trader, association, or parts or combination thereof.

NOTE 1   The arrangement is generally orderly.

NOTE 2   An organization can be public or private.

NOTE 3   This definition is valid for the purposes of **quality management system** (3.2.3) standards. The term "organization" is defined differently in ISO/IEC Guide 2.

Process (3.4.1)—set of interrelated or interacting activities which transforms inputs into outputs

NOTE 1   Inputs to a process are generally outputs of other processes.

NOTE 2   Processes in an **organization** (3.3.1) are generally planned and carried out under controlled conditions to add value.

NOTE 3   A process where the **conformity** (3.6.1) of the resulting **product** (3.4.2) cannot be readily or economically verified is frequently referred to as a "special process".

Quality management system (3.2.3)—**management system** (3.2.2) to direct and control an **organization** (3.3.1) with regard to **quality** (3.1.1)

Quality objective (3.2.5)—something sought, or aimed for, related to **quality** (3.1.1)

NOTE 1   Quality objectives are generally based on the organization's **quality policy** (3.2.4).

NOTE 2   Quality objectives are generally specified for relevant functions and levels in the **organization** (3.3.1).

Quality policy (3.2.4)—overall intentions and direction of an **organization** (3.3.1) related to **quality** (3.1.1) as formally expressed by **top management** (3.2.7)

NOTE 1   Generally the quality policy is consistent with the overall policy of the organization and provides a framework for the setting of **quality objectives** (3.2.5).

NOTE 2   Quality management principles presented in this International Standard can form a basis for the establishment of a quality policy. (See 0.2.)

Source: ANSI/ISO/ASQ Q9000-2000

 # TYPICAL AUDIT ITEMS FOR COMPLIANCE

Items representing a difference from ISO 9001:1994 have a Δ at the end.

- Does the organization plan and manage processes necessary for the continual improvement of the quality management system? Δ

- Does the organization use quality policy, quality objectives, and data analysis to facilitate the continual improvement of the quality management system? Δ

- Does the organization use audit results, corrective action, and preventive action to facilitate the continual improvement of the quality management system?

8.5.2 Corrective action

The organization shall take action to eliminate the cause of nonconformities in order to prevent recurrence. Corrective actions shall be appropriate to the effects of the nonconformities encountered.

A documented procedure shall be established to define requirements for

a) reviewing nonconformities (including customer complaints),

b) determining the causes of nonconformities,

c) evaluating the need for action to ensure that nonconformities do not recur,

d) determining and implementing action needed,

e) records of the results of action taken (see 4.2.4), and

f) reviewing corrective action taken.

Source: ANSI/ISO/ASQ Q9001-2000

The corrective action concept has been a part of ISO 9001 from the beginning. It involves taking action to eliminate the causes of nonconformities.

Nonconformities must be identified in some manner so that the system can deal with them. This does not relate to the physical identification and disposition of nonconforming material covered in clause 8.3. Requirements for customer communications in clause 7.2.3 state that arrangements must be made with customers relating to complaints. Clause 8.5.2 requires the identification of nonconformities to include these customer complaints. ISO 9001:1994, in clause 4.14.2, has a similar requirement for "the effective handling of customer complaints and reports of nonconformities." The words "effective handling" do not appear in ISO 9001:2000, since it is fundamental that all parts of the quality management system must be effective.

The requirements for determining the causes of nonconformities and complaints must be specified in a documented procedure. Organizations should focus the process on determining *root causes.* There must be a process to evaluate the need for actions to ensure that nonconformities do not recur. In some cases, action may neither be required nor appropriate. If the nonconformity is minor and an isolated condition, the risks or cost associated with taking corrective action may not be justified. Without this determination, resources may be diverted from the identification and correction of the more important customer complaints and nonconformities. It is fundamental that the corrective actions taken be appropriate to the nature of the problem.

Nonconformities need to be evaluated, and the root causes of their occurrence need to be determined. Evaluations of the nonconformities should indicate what corrective actions to take to eliminate the root causes of the nonconformities.

 Once action to correct the cause of the nonconformity has been determined, it needs to be implemented. The corrective action process must also provide for recording the results of the corrective actions taken. In ISO 9001:1994, clause 4.14.2d required the "application of controls to ensure that corrective action is taken and that it is effective." In many organizations, a sign-off by someone who reviews the action taken and judges the effectiveness has been used to meet this requirement. The new standard is a bit more prescriptive in that the actual results of the corrective action must be recorded.

If actual results are recorded, the review for effectiveness can be conducted in a more objective manner. Review is required to ensure that the corrective actions have been implemented and are effective in preventing the problem from recurring.

SERVICES, HARDWARE, PROCESSED MATERIALS, AND SOFTWARE

The practices required to comply with the general management clauses are essentially identical regardless of the category of product.

 # DEFINITIONS

Corrective action (3.6.5)—action to eliminate the cause of a detected **nonconformity** (3.6.2) or other undesirable situation

NOTE 1   There can be more than one cause for a nonconformity.

NOTE 2   Corrective action is taken to prevent recurrence whereas **preventive action** (3.6.4) is taken to prevent occurrence.

NOTE 3   There is a distinction between **correction** (3.6.6) and corrective action.

Customer (3.3.5)—**organization** (3.3.1) or person that receives a **product** (3.4.2)

EXAMPLE   Consumer, client, end-user, retailer, beneficiary and purchaser.

NOTE   A customer can be internal or external to the organization.

Nonconformity (3.6.2)—non-fulfilment of a **requirement** (3.1.2)

Requirement (3.1.2)—need or expectation that is stated, generally implied or obligatory

NOTE 1   "Generally implied" means that it is custom or common practice for the **organization** (3.3.1), its **customers** (3.3.5) and other **interested parties** (3.3.7), that the need or expectation under consideration is implied.

NOTE 2   A qualifier can be used to denote a specific type of requirement, e.g. product requirement, quality management requirement, customer requirement.

NOTE 3   A specified requirement is one which is stated, for example, in a **document** (3.7.2).

NOTE 4   Requirements can be generated by different interested parties.

Review (3.8.7)—activity undertaken to determine the suitability, adequacy and **effectiveness** (3.2.14) of the subject matter to achieve established objectives

NOTE   Review can also include the determination of **efficiency** (3.2.15).
EXAMPLE   Management review, design and development review, review of customer requirements and nonconformity review.

Source: ANSI/ISO/ASQ Q9000-2000

CONSIDERATIONS FOR DOCUMENTATION

Clause 8.5.2 specifically requires a documented procedure for corrective action, and the procedure must provide for specific listed activities. This clause requires the recording of the results of corrective action. There is also a specific reference to clause 4.2.4 for control of the records generated. Organizations should maintain records of corrective actions required, root causes found, actions taken, results of the actions, and review of the results to ensure that the action was effective.

TYPICAL AUDIT ITEMS FOR COMPLIANCE

Items representing a difference from ISO 9001:1994 have a Δ at the end.

• Does the organization take corrective action to eliminate the causes of nonconformities?

• Is the corrective action taken appropriate to the impact of the problems encountered?

• Do documented procedures for corrective action provide for identifying nonconformities, determining causes, evaluating the need for actions to prevent recurrence, determining the corrective action needed, and the implementation of the needed corrective action?

• Do documented procedures for corrective action provide for recording the results of corrective actions taken? Δ

• Do the documented procedures for corrective action provide for reviewing the corrective action taken?

8.5.3 Preventive action

The organization shall determine action to eliminate the causes of potential nonconformities in order to prevent their occurrence. Preventive actions shall be appropriate to the effects of the potential problems.

A documented procedure shall be established to define requirements for

a) determining potential nonconformities and their causes,

b) evaluating the need for action to prevent occurrence of nonconformities,

c) determining and implementing action needed,

d) records of results of action taken (see 4.2.4), and

e) reviewing preventive action taken.

Source: ANSI/ISO/ASQ Q9001-2000

The concept of preventive action was added to ISO 9001 in the 1994 revision and the preventive action requirements in ISO 9001:2000 are not intended to be different from the 1994 version. Many organizations do not separate the concepts and use the same process for both corrective action and preventive action. Actually, the concepts are somewhat different and the techniques are different for each. While corrective action involves the solving of known problems, preventive action is intended to identify the potential causes of problems. In preventive action the organization is required to identify how it will eliminate the "causes" of potential nonconformities in order to prevent their occurrence.

It is not intended that the organization identify every possible nonconformity that could be envisioned, but there must be a defined method to identify those for which the organization chooses to take preventive action. Organizations have the freedom to define this in a manner that best suits their business situation. There are a number of ways to identify potential problems and to assess their potential impact. Some examples include the following:

- When nonconformities are identified in one part of the organization and causes are addressed by the corrective action system, some organizations look for similar situations in other areas. For example, if action is taken to correct the cause of a nonconformity for one product line, it may be wise to determine if similar nonconformities are likely for other lines. If so, preventive action may be appropriate for the other lines.

- Risk analysis or failure modes and effects analysis may be used to identify potential problems and to assess their potential impacts.

- The analysis of data on process performance may identify process parameters that have a high probability of creating nonconformities.

- Management review may be used as a vehicle for discussing and evaluating areas for preventive actions.

The documented procedure must also provide for determining and ensuring the implementation of preventive actions to eliminate the potential causes identified.

 As with corrective action, ISO 9001:2000 requires that the results of the preventive actions taken be recorded. In many organizations, a sign-off by someone who reviews the action taken and judges the effectiveness has been used to meet this requirement. The new standard is a bit more prescriptive in that the actual results of the preventive action must be recorded. If actual results are recorded, the review for effectiveness can be conducted in a more objective manner. This implies that there will be some information or data recorded to verify that the potential nonconformity has not occurred over some reasonable time period. Review is required to ensure that the preventive actions have been implemented and are effective in preventing the potential problem from occurring.

SERVICES, HARDWARE, PROCESSED MATERIALS, AND SOFTWARE

The practices required to comply with the general management clauses are essentially identical regardless of the category of product.

 DEFINITIONS

Nonconformity (3.6.2)—non-fulfilment of a **requirement** (3.1.2)

Preventive action (3.6.4)—action to eliminate the cause of a potential **nonconformity** (3.6.2) or other undesirable potential situation

NOTE 1   There can be more than one cause for a potential nonconformity.

NOTE 2   Preventive action is taken to prevent occurrence whereas **corrective action** (3.6.5) is taken to prevent recurrence.

Requirement (3.1.2)—need or expectation that is stated, generally implied or obligatory

NOTE 1   "Generally implied" means that it is custom or common practice for the **organization** (3.3.1), its **customers** (3.3.5) and other **interested parties** (3.3.7), that the need or expectation under consideration is implied.

NOTE 2   A qualifier can be used to denote a specific type of requirement, e.g. product requirement, quality management requirement, customer requirement.

NOTE 3   A specified requirement is one which is stated, for example, in a **document** (3.7.2).

NOTE 4   Requirements can be generated by different interested parties.

Review (3.8.7)—activity undertaken to determine the suitability, adequacy and **effectiveness** (3.2.14) of the subject matter to achieve established objectives

NOTE   Review can also include the determination of **efficiency** (3.2.15).

EXAMPLE   Management review, design and development review, review of customer requirements and nonconformity review.

Source: ANSI/ISO/ASQ Q9000-2000

CONSIDERATIONS FOR DOCUMENTATION

As with corrective action, the organization is required to have a documented procedure to define specific activities. Clause 8.5.3 requires records of preventive action results with specific reference to clause 5.5.7 for control of the records generated. Organizations should consider maintaining records of preventive action projects undertaken, potential root causes found, actions taken, results of the actions, and review of the results to ensure that the action was effective.

 TYPICAL AUDIT ITEMS FOR COMPLIANCE

Items representing a difference from ISO 9001:1994 have a Δ at the end.

• Does the organization identify preventive actions needed to eliminate the potential causes of possible nonconformities?

• Is preventive action taken appropriate to the impact of potential problems?

• Do the documented procedures for preventive action provide for identifying potential nonconformities and their probable causes?

• Do the documented procedures for preventive action provide for determining the need for preventive action and the implementation of the preventive action needed?

• Do the documented procedures for preventive action provide for recording the results of the preventive actions taken? Δ

• Do the documented procedures for preventive action provide for reviewing the preventive action taken?

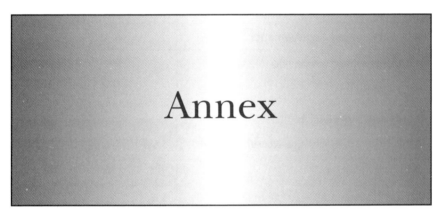

Annex

Note: This annex is Annex B of ANSI/ISO/ASQ Q9001-2000.

ANNEX B
(informative)

Correspondence between ISO 9001:2000 and ISO 9001:1994

Table B.1   Correspondence between ISO 9001:1994
and ISO 9001:2000

ISO 9001:1994	ISO 9001:2000
1 Scope	1
2 Normative reference	2
3 Definitions	3
4 Quality system requirements [title only]	
4.1 Management responsibility [title only]	
4.1.1 Quality policy	5.1 + 5.3 + 5.4.1
4.1.2 Organization [title only]	
4.1.2.1 Responsibility and authority	5.5.1
4.1.2.2 Resources	6.1 + 6.2.1
4.1.2.3 Management representative	5.5.2
4.1.3 Management review	5.6.1 + 8.5.1
4.2 Quality system [title only]	
4.2.1 General	4.1 + 4.2.2
4.2.2 Quality system procedures	4.2.1
4.2.3 Quality planning	5.4.2 + 7.1
4.3 Contract review [title only]	
4.3.1 General	
4.3.2 Review	5.2 + 7.2.1 + 7.2.2 + 7.2.3
4.3.3 Amendment to a contract	7.2.2
4.3.4 Records	7.2.2

(Continued)

Table B.1   Continued.

ISO 9001:1994	ISO 9001:2000
4.4 Design control [title only]	
4.4.1 General	
4.4.2 Design and development planning	7.3.1
4.4.3 Organizational and technical interfaces	7.3.1
4.4.4 Design input	7.2.1 + 7.3.2
4.4.5 Design output	7.3.3
4.4.6 Design review	7.3.4
4.4.7 Design verification	7.3.5
4.4.8 Design validation	7.3.6
4.4.9 Design changes	7.3.7
4.5 Document and data control [title only]	
4.5.1 General	4.2.3
4.5.2 Document and data approval and issue	4.2.3
4.5.3 Document and data changes	4.2.3
4.6 Purchasing [title only]	
4.6.1 General	
4.6.2 Evaluation of subcontractors	7.4.1
4.6.3 Purchasing data	7.4.2
4.6.4 Verification of purchased product	7.4.3
4.7 Control of customer-supplied product	7.5.4
4.8 Product identification and traceability	7.5.3
4.9 Process control	6.3 + 6.4 + 7.5.1 + 7.5.2

(Continued)

Table B.1   Continued.

ISO 9001:1994	ISO 9001:2000
4.10 Inspection and testing [title only]	
4.10.1 General	7.1 + 8.1
4.10.2 Receiving inspection and testing	7.4.3 + 8.2.4
4.10.3 In-process inspection and testing	8.2.4
4.10.4 Final inspection and testing	8.2.4
4.10.5 Inspection and test records	7.5.3 + 8.2.4
4.11 Control of inspection, measuring and test equipment [title only]	
4.11.1 General	7.6
4.11.2 Control procedure	7.6
4.12 Inspection and test status	7.5.3
4.13 Control of nonconforming product [title only]	
4.13.1 General	8.3
4.13.2 Review and disposition of nonconforming product	8.3
4.14 Corrective and preventive action [title only]	
4.14.1 General	8.5.2 + 8.5.3
4.14.2 Corrective action	8.5.2
4.14.3 Preventive action	8.5.3

(Continued)

Table B.1 Continued.

ISO 9001:1994	ISO 9001:2000
4.15 Handling, storage, packaging, preservation & delivery [title only]	
4.15.1 General	
4.15.2 Handling	7.5.5
4.15.3 Storage	7.5.5
4.15.4 Packaging	7.5.5
4.15.5 Preservation	7.5.5
4.15.6 Delivery	7.5.1
4.16 Control of quality records	4.2.4
4.17 Internal quality audits	8.2.2 + 8.2.3
4.18 Training	6.2.2
4.19 Servicing	7.5.1
4.20 Statistical techniques [title only]	
4.20.1 Identification of need	8.1 + 8.2.3 + 8.2.4 + 8.4
4.20.2 Procedures	8.1 + 8.2.3 + 8.2.4 + 8.4

Source: ANSI/ISO/ASQ Q9001-2000

Table B.2   Correspondence between ISO 9001:2000
and ISO 9001:1994

ISO 9001:2000	ISO 9001:1994
1 Scope	**1**
1.1 General	
1.2 Application	
2 Normative reference	**2**
3 Terms and definitions	**3**
4 Quality management system [title only]	
4.1 General requirements	4.2.1
4.2 Documentation requirements [title only]	
4.2.1 General	4.2.2
4.2.2 Quality manual	4.2.1
4.2.3 Control of documents	4.5.1 + 4.5.2 + 4.5.3
4.2.4 Control of records	4.16
5 Management responsibility [title only]	
5.1 Management commitment	4.1.1
5.2 Customer focus	4.3.2
5.3 Quality policy	4.1.1
5.4 Planning [title only]	
5.4.1 Quality objectives	4.1.1
5.4.2 Quality management system planning	4.2.3
5.5 Responsibility, authority and communication [title only]	
5.5.1 Responsibility and authority	4.1.2.1

(Continued)

Table B.2   Continued.

ISO 9001:2000	ISO 9001:1994
5.5.2 Management representative 5.5.3 Internal communication	4.1.2.3
5.6 Management review [title only] 5.6.1 General 5.6.2 Review input 5.6.3 Review output	 4.1.3
6 Resource management [title only]	
6.1 Provision of resources	4.1.2.2
6.2 Human resources [title only] 6.2.1 General	 4.1.2.2
6.2.2 Competence, awareness and training	4.18
6.3 Infrastructure	4.9
6.4 Work environment	4.9
7 Product realization [title only]	
7.1 Planning of product realization	4.2.3 + 4.10.1
7.2 Customer-related processes [title only]	
7.2.1 Determination of requirements related to the product	4.3.2 + 4.4.4
7.2.2 Review of requirements related to the product	4.3.2 + 4.3.3 + 4.3.4
7.2.3 Customer communication	4.3.2
7.3 Design and development [title only] 7.3.1 Design and development planning	 4.4.2 + 4.4.3
7.3.2 Design and development inputs	4.4.4

(Continued)

Table B.2   Continued.

ISO 9001:2000	ISO 9001:1994
7.3.3 Design and development outputs	4.4.5
7.3.4 Design and development review	4.4.6
7.3.5 Design and development verification	4.4.7
7.3.6 Design and development validation	4.4.8
7.3.7 Control of design and development changes	4.4.9
7.4 Purchasing [title only]	
7.4.1 Purchasing process	4.6.2
7.4.2 Purchasing information	4.6.3
7.4.3 Verification of purchased product	4.6.4 + 4.10.2
7.5 Production and service provision [title only]	
7.5.1 Control of production and service provision	4.9 + 4.15.6 + 4.19
7.5.2 Validation of processes for production and service provision	4.9
7.5.3 Identification and traceability	4.8 + 4.10.5 + 4.12
7.5.4 Customer property	4.7
7.5.5 Preservation of product	4.15.2 + 4.15.3 + 4.15.4 + 4.15.5
7.6 Control of monitoring and measuring devices	4.11.1 + 4.11.2
8 Measurement, analysis and improvement [title only]	
8.1 General	4.10.1 + 4.20.1 + 4.20.2

(Continued)

Table B.2   Continued.

ISO 9001:2000	ISO 9001:1994
8.2 Monitoring and measurement [title only]	
8.2.1 Customer satisfaction	
8.2.2 Internal audit	4.17
8.2.3 Monitoring and measurement of processes	4.17 + 4.20.1 + 4.20.2
8.2.4 Monitoring and measurement of product	4.10.2 + 4.10.3 + 4.10.4 + 4.10.5 + 4.20.1 + 4.20.2
8.3 Control of nonconformity product	4.13.1 + 4.13.2
8.4 Analysis of data	4.20.1 + 4.20.2
8.5 Improvement [title only]	
8.5.1 Continual improvement	4.1.3
8.5.2 Corrective action	4.14.1 + 4.14.2
8.5.3 Preventive action	4.14.1 + 4.14.3

Index